1001 FACTS THAT WILL BLOW YOUR MIND

QANA BOOKS

FOREWORD

We love facts. The more awe-inspiring the better.
So, we have put together a 1001 of the most
interesting and unusual facts we could find.
Whether you are looking for a fun way to pass
the time or seeking to expand your knowledge
and understanding of the world around you,
there is a plethora of trivia here to entertain and
enlighten you.
We hope you will be amazed, amused, and
intrigued by the facts and events you are about to
read.

CONTENTS

SPACE

Space starts at the Kármán line, which is only 100 kilometers, or 62 miles, above mean sea level.

Zero gravity does not exist. Anything with mass has gravitational attraction. Astronauts are weightless because everything in orbit is in free fall towards the Earth at the same speed. When in orbit, astronauts experience 90% of Earth's gravity.

If you end up in space without a spacesuit, you will not freeze, boil, or explode. You would die from suffocation, however.

Flying through an asteroid field is not as dangerous as the movies would have you believe. The average distance between asteroids in an asteroid field is about two million kilometers.

The moon has gravity, but it is only 17% of the gravity we have on Earth.

From Earth, the color of the sun is dependent on atmospheric conditions, but despite it technically being a yellow star, our sun is white.

The heat of the sun is produced by nuclear fusion rather than chemical combustion, so it is not on fire or burning, and what look like flames are called prominences, made of plasma, helium, and hydrogen.

On Jupiter and Saturn, it rains tiny diamonds.

Moon dust smells of burnt gunpowder according to Apollo astronauts who have been there.

There is no such thing as the dark side of the moon. The moon is tidally locked to the Earth, so we only see one side, but all sides of the moon receive the same amount of sunlight.

In January 2014, emissions of water vapor were detected around Ceres, a dwarf planet in the asteroid belt between the orbits of Mars and Jupiter.

Sputnik 1 was the first artificial satellite. But it wasn't the first man-made object to reach space. That was a V2 rocket launched on October 3, 1942, from Germany.

Venus is hotter than Mercury despite Mercury being closer to the Sun and Neptune is warmer than Uranus despite being further from the Sun.

It takes an average 200,000 years for photons to travel from the Sun's core to its surface and just over eight minutes to travel from the surface to the Earth.

One of Uranus's moons is called Margaret.

96% of the universe is missing.

The Earth's rotation rate slows at a rate of 0.005 seconds per year per year.

If two pieces of the same type of metal touch in space they will permanently bond, in an effect known as cold welding.

There is water floating in space. A recently discovered cloud of water vapor is estimated to contain at least 140 trillion times the amount of water in all the oceans on Earth.

Olympus Mons on Mars is the highest peak on any planet, two and a half times the height of Everest, but the Rheasilva Peak on the asteroid Vesta is even higher.

Einstein and Quantum theory predict the existence of White Holes as the exit point of matter sucked into a black hole.

In 1976 the Viking mission to Mars returned positive results for life in one of its experiments. They were discounted because other tests did not support those results. It's now argued by many that it was the other tests that were flawed.

Astronomers have found evidence suggesting there is a ninth Neptune sized planet beyond Pluto in our solar system.

An oblong shaped object between 100 and 1000 meters long named 'Oumuamua was the first interstellar object detected passing through our Solar System. Its shape, origin, acceleration, and mass made some astronomers suggest that it could be alien technology.

Saturn's moon Iapetus has a raised ridge higher than Mount Everest that runs perfectly around its equator. Astronomers have no credible explanation as to why or how it got there.

The Milky Way gets a new star every 50 days.

Saturn has a persistent hexagonal shaped storm and astronomers do not really know why it is that shape.

The Great Attractor is a region of space with a massive gravitational pull that is attracting hundreds of galaxy clusters, including our Milky Way, towards it. Despite intense study, its exact nature remains a mystery.

The area code for Cape Canaveral is 3-2-1.

The Sun is so large that it accounts for 99.86% of the mass in our solar system.

There is a United Nations Office for Outer Space Affairs.

Pioneer 10 and Pioneer 11, two NASA probes launched in the 1970's, are changing speed and trajectory for no known reason.

Transient Lunar Phenomena are short-lived changes in the appearance of the Moon's surface that can include bright flashes of light, changes in the color or brightness of certain areas, or the sudden appearance or disappearance of features. Though reported for centuries they are still not understood.

On August 15, 1977, a strong, narrow-band radio emission that lasted for 72 seconds was detected from space. It was so distinctive that astronomer Jerry Ehman wrote "Wow!" on the computer printout. Though it seemed artificial it has not been detected since.

Sunsets on Mars are blue.

An estimated 180 metric tons of human garbage
has been left on the moon.

Neil Armstrong's NASA application arrived a
week after the closing deadline.

Humans have caused global warming on the
Moon. According to one study, the astronauts
who walked on the moon kicked aside so much
dust that the darker soil underneath, exposed for
the first time in billions of years, absorbed
enough solar radiation to raise the temperature of
the moon's surface by up to 3.6°F (2°C).

Astronaut Scott Kelly spent 11 months in space.
When he returned, he was thirteen milliseconds
younger than his identical twin brother.

All galaxies rotate once about every billion years, regardless of their size.

Tabby's Star is a star that is located about 1,500 light-years away that has unique fluctuations in brightness, the exact cause of which remains a mystery.

Despite temperatures reaching 800°F (430°C) on Mercury, it still has ice at or near its surface.

Mercury and Venus have no moons, and astronomers are not sure why.

The farthest object visible with the naked eye is the Andromeda galaxy, 2.7 million light years away.

Galaxy LEDA 074886 is rectangular like a cut emerald.

The Earth spins at 1,000mph but it travels through space at 67,000mph.

Fast Radio Bursts are brief, intense bursts of radio waves that last just a few milliseconds. They were first discovered in 2007 and their origin remains one of the biggest mysteries in astronomy.

The Earth is 4.56 billion years old, the same age as the Moon and the Sun.

The International Space Station is closer to the earth than San Francisco is to L.A.

The Sun is about four hundred times larger than the Moon, but also about four hundred times farther away from Earth which is why we can experience total solar eclipses. It is a unique combination in our solar system.

ANIMALS

Starfish can re-grow their arms and, in some cases, entire bodies.

Seahorses are monogamous life mates.

Blue whales cannot swallow anything bigger than a grapefruit.

Sea cucumbers eat with their feet.

A manatee's nipples are in its armpits.

Nobody has ever seen European Eels mate in the wild.

There is, genetically speaking, no such thing as a fish. What we call fish are so genetically different that some are more closely related to humans than they are other 'fish'.

Goldfish have a memory of at least three months and can learn to recognize faces.

There are nine known species of walking shark, one of which can walk outside of water.

90% of all jellyfish are smaller than a thumbnail.

Whales can only taste salt.

An Atlantic salmon's sense of smell is a thousand times better than a dog's.

Dolphins only allow half their brains to sleep at a time so that they continue to surface to breathe.

Fish can yawn and cough.

The strike of a mantis shrimp is so fast it makes the surrounding water boil.

Mantis shrimp can see a type of light no other animal can, called circularly polarized light.

Sea urchins are the only animals that can see despite not having eyes. They use their feet instead.

The Upside-down catfish swims upside down. And no one knows why.

Greenland sharks do not reach sexual maturity until they are 150 years old and have the longest known lifespan of any vertebrate on the planet, reaching an age of 400.

The Turritopsis Dohrnii Jellyfish can revert to its juvenile polyp stage after maturing in an endless cycle that makes it the only known biologically immortal creature.

Snails are getting slower, and scientists are not sure why.

There is an ecosystem of termites underneath northeastern Brazil which is as large as Great Britain and some parts are thought to be nearly 4,000 years old.

There are species of ants that will defend their colony by exploding suicidally, spraying a toxic chemical on the attackers.

95% of house spiders never go outside.

No centipede has ever been found to have exactly one hundred legs despite the name.

Ants have two stomachs, one for themselves and one for sharing with other ants that haven't found any food.

When Earthworms mate, they both have children.

The Greater Wax moth can hear sounds that are higher pitched than any animal is known to make.

Spider silk conducts heat as well as or better than most metals.

Giant Himalayan bees make what is called "mad honey", a powerful hallucinogen that is used as a recreational drug.

There are bees called Vulture Bees that feed on, and make honey from, rotten meat.

The giant honeybees of East Asia build open nests that are attractive to predators, so they employ a technique called shimmering that is like a Mexican wave where hundreds of the bees work in unison shaking their rear-ends. How they communicate to produce this highly coordinated response remains unknown.

If an earthworm is split in two, it will not become two new worms. It may survive and regenerate a new tail. However, the Planarian Flatworm can reform its entire body from a sliver including regrowing a head that retains all its old memories.

Human tapeworms can grow up to 22.9 meters.

Bees have knees.

ManhattAnts are an ant species unique to New York City.

The world's smallest wasp, the Megaphragma mymaripenne wasp, is smaller than an amoeba.

Every spring, the fireflies of the Great Smoky Mountains National Park in the United States flash entirely in unison, in bursts that can last for hours.

Male flies produce a substance that makes females sleep after mating, reducing the chances that they will go on to mate with another fly.

Coconut crabs climb trees and hunt birds.

A bite from a Russell's Pit viper can send the victim back through puberty permanently.

Lizards cannot breathe and walk at the same time.

There are species of lizards and of fish that are warm blooded.

The salamander can regenerate lost limbs, damaged lungs, a sliced spinal cord, and parts of its brain.

Salamanders use their lungs to hear.

Alligators and crocodiles having a massive bite strength of 2000 to 5000 psi. But you can keep their jaws shut with a rubber band.

Chameleons change color according to their emotions and not to blend in with their background.

To achieve the best possible camouflage when it sleeps, the Glass Frog stores its red blood cells in its liver.

Moles shrink their brains in winter to conserve energy.

The wild dogs of Botswana use sneezing to vote
on whether to initiate a hunt.

Goats have rectangular pupils.

There are more tigers in captivity in the United
States than there are roaming free in the wild.

Dogs can smell cancer.

Wombat feces are cube shaped.

Lemmings do not jump off cliffs to their deaths.

Elephants really do have incredible memories.

Coyotes in the US have learnt how traffic lights work and which way traffic flows. In fact, they will only look in one direction on a one-way road.

Grapes are poisonous to dogs as are avocados to horses.

Camels originated in North America.

Humans, mice, and giraffes have the same number of neck vertebrae: Seven.

Bulls cannot see the color red.

Rats are ticklish.

Camels do not store water in their humps.

Cows with names produce up to five percent more milk than cows without a name.

Polar Bears are not white, their fur is translucent, and only appears white because it reflects visible light.

Hamsters blink one eye at a time.

A Monkey trained to use currency used it for prostitution.

An animal the size of a wolf, that looks like a fox and has a mane like a lion, roams countries in South America. Although it is called a Maned wolf, it is in fact the largest canine in South America.

The longest beaver dam in the world is 850m (2,788 ft) long and is in Wood Buffalo Park in Alberta, Canada.

The Myanmar snub-nosed monkey sneezes uncontrollably when it rains.

Cows moo in different regional accents.

Mice are stressed by the smell of men but not women.

Polar bears cannot be seen using night vision equipment.

Black leopards have spots, but they can only be seen in infrared light.

The kangaroo mouse never needs to drink water.

Pandas are losing their black eye patches, and scientists don't know why.

Adult cats only meow at humans and not each other.

Species of reindeer, known as Rangifer tarandus, native to some Arctic regions, actually do have red noses.

Placebos work on dogs.

Armadillos almost always give birth to identical quadruplets.

The patterns on a giraffe are totally unique to it.

Domestic cats and some species of big cats, purr at frequencies optimal for pain relief and even bone repair.

A horse can output up to 15 horsepower.

Of all the deadly animals in the world (that are not a mosquito), if you are in Africa, hippopotamuses are the deadliest, it's snakes in South America while the animal that kills the most people in North America is the deer.

Pigs can be taught to control joysticks with their snouts to steer a cursor on screen that can win them treats.

The Malabar Giant Squirrel is a giant technicolored squirrel.

Apes who have been taught sign language have not demonstrated an ability to ask questions about new knowledge.

In the Samburu national park in northern Kenya there was a lioness called Kamuniak, who over the course of her life adopted at least six baby oryx instead of eating them.

A chicken can live for 2 years without a head.

The egg came before the chicken because chickens evolved from reptiles who were already laying eggs.

An active hummingbird's heart rate is 1,200 beats per minute.

Ravens in captivity can learn to talk better than parrots.

Pigeons see at 250 frames per second, humans see at 30-60 fps.

Ostriches do not bury their head in the sand when scared.

Ayam Cemani chickens are entirely black including feathers, beak, and internal organs.

The Robin Redbreast is called that despite its distinctive orange colored breast because it was named before the existence of orange as a color name in the English language.

The longest animal migration on record is the annual migration of the Arctic tern, which can fly up to 25,000 miles (40,000km) per year.

Flamingos are born grey or white. They turn pink because of the pigments found in the algae and invertebrates that they eat.

Flamingos bend their legs at the ankle, not the knee.

In 1932, the Australian army went to 'war' with a pack of Emus in Western Australia, twice. The emus survived.

GEOGRAPHY

Mount Everest has the highest peak on Earth measured from sea level but due to the bulge in the Earth at the Equator, Ecuador's Mount Chimborazo is 2,072 meters further from the center of the Earth than Everest and closer to space.

Mount Kilimanjaro is the tallest single free-standing mountain on Earth, while Mauna Kea, which starts below sea level is about 4,000 feet taller than Mount Everest.

There are no tides. There is a bulge of water caused by the pull of the Sun and the Moon, and the Earth rotates through that bulge.

Planet Earth vibrates every 27 seconds and geologists have no idea what is causing it.

The western flank of the of the Cumbre Vieja volcano on the island of La Palma in the Canary Islands measures around 1.5 trillion metric tons in volume. Were it to collapse all at once, it would cause a tsunami which would be at least fifty meters high when it hit Western Europe and North America.

You can drive from Norway to North Korea just by driving through Russia.

Iceland widens by 2cm every year.

Canada and the Philippines have the only known examples of third order islands: That is an island that sits in a lake that is on an island that sits in a lake that is on an island.

Bir Tawil is a 2,060 km2 (795.4 sq mi) area of land along the border between Egypt and Sudan. It is uninhabited and claimed by neither country.

The Chamarel plain in Mauritius has a small area of sand dunes made up of sand in seven distinct colors.

Son Doong cave in Vietnam has the largest known cross-section of any cave in the world. It is so large that it has its own vegetation, fast flowing river, and weather system.

Edinburgh is on the east coast of Britain but is further west than Liverpool which is on the west coast of Britain.

Reno in inland Nevada is 86 miles further west than the west coast city of Los Angeles.

Toronto, in Canada, is further south than London, Paris, Berlin, and Milan.

The beautiful tropical white sand that makes up picture postcard beaches is almost entirely parrotfish droppings.

Tens of square kilometers of the eastern Sahara are littered with glass the origin of which is uncertain.

There is a rainforest 50% bigger than the Amazon that stretches across the northern hemisphere called the boreal forest or taiga.

Vinicunca Mountain is a mountain in the Andes of Peru made up of different layers of sediment of many different colors. It was only discovered to look that way in 2015 when the snow covering it melted.

The transition zone of the Earth's interior, located between the upper and lower mantle, is totally different to the other layers in almost every way and scientists are not sure why.

Before, during, or after earthquakes, people have reported bright flashes of light, balls of fire, or a luminous glow in the sky. On-going research has not managed to solve their origin.

You weigh less if you visit certain areas of Canada, such as Hudson Bay and parts of Quebec, because there is less gravity there than other parts of the world.

Ball lightning is a rare and mysterious weather phenomenon, characterized by the appearance of a glowing ball of light, ranging in size from a few centimeters to a meter, that floats in the air for several seconds or minutes before disappearing. Scientists are still not entirely sure what causes it.

The soil in your garden is 2 million years old.

Snow at the south pole reflects sound so well, you can hear people talking a mile away.

Lebanon in the Middle East has more average annual rainfall than the United Kingdom.

There is an eighth continent called Zealandia but 94% of it is underwater.

The upper atmosphere is full of bacteria and some scientists believe they can affect weather patterns.

Water is blue, not transparent.

The tallest tree ever recorded was a 379.7-foot (115.7-meter) tall coast redwood named Hyperion.

The oldest known tree in the world is a bristlecone pine tree in the White Mountains of California that is over 5,000 years old.

Baku, the capital Azerbaijan, is 28 meters below sea level.

The majority of the Sahara Desert is gravel, not sand.

The largest living organism in the world is a fungus called Armillaria ostoyae, which covers 2,200 acres (890 hectares) of the Blue Mountains in Oregon, USA.

Trees have a pulse they use to pump water.

Trees sweat.

Australia is wider than the moon by 600km.

There are still an estimated ten million mammoths trapped in the arctic permafrost.

France's longest border is with Brazil.

Canary birds are named after the Canary Islands which are named after their Latin name Canariae Insulae, or "Islands of the Dogs."

American tree populations are moving west. No one knows why.

Oceans are getting louder because there is less ice to absorb the noise and warmer waters allow sound waves to travel faster and farther.

The average cloud weighs around 551 tons.

The 2011 Japan earthquake knocked 1.8 microseconds off our days. The 2004 Sumatra quake cost us 6.8 microseconds.

Australia is moving north by 2.7 inches a year.

There are rainforests in Europe and Perućica in Bosnia Herzegovina is Europe's largest.

The highest drivable road in the world is in Khardung La in Tibet. The road sits at an elevation of 5,359 meters.

40% to 50% of the all the gold ever mined has come came from a single plateau in South Africa called Witwatersrand.

There is only one species of tea plant.

If an underwater bubble is collapsed by sound, light is produced and there are competing theories why.

The smell of freshly cut grass is a distress call to alert other plants to imminent danger.

A teaspoon of soil in the Amazon contains 400 different fungal species.

The world's largest waterfall is underwater. At the Denmark Strait, the freezing water from the Nordic Sea is denser than the Irminger Sea's warm water, making it drop almost 3,500 meters (11,500 feet) at 123 million cubic feet per second.

The driest place on Earth is in Antarctica in an area called the Dry Valleys, which has seen no rain or moisture for nearly two million years.

It is often said that no two snowflakes can be the same. However, in 1988, Nancy Knight, a scientist at the National Center for Atmosphere Research in Colorado, USA, found two identical snowflakes while studying snow crystals.

Hurricanes with female names are deadlier than ones with male names. Scientists believe this is because the name leads to a lower perceived risk.

Gigantic jet lightning are powerful bursts of electrical charge, ten times larger than normal lightning, that fire upwards out the tops of clouds.

The city of Iquitos in Peru has a population of over 400,000 but is not reachable by road.

There is an effect called fata morgana which is an atmospheric effect caused by a temperature inversion. It bends light so that an entire city scape can appear to float in the sky.

The highest recorded temperature on Earth was 134°F (56.7°C), recorded at the Furnace Creek Ranch in Death Valley, California, USA on July 10, 1913.

The construction of the Three Gorges Dam in China caused such a significant redistribution of water when it was built, that it slowed the world's rotation by 0.06 microseconds and moved the poles by 2cm.

There is a rare type of rock called Itacolumite that is naturally bendable.

Africa is slowly splitting in two along a tectonic plate boundary known as the East African Rift System.

Providence Canyon State Park in Georgia in the USA is a 150-foot-deep canyon that was formed due to poor farming practices in the 19th century.

The Earth's magnetic North Pole used to have an average annual drift of around 10-15 kilometers per year in the early 20th century. However, in recent years, it has been moving and accelerating at a much faster rate of approximately 50-60 kilometers per year.

For over a hundred years an island the size of Manhattan, called Sandy Island, in the Pacific Ocean, northwest of Australia, has appeared on maps. It even found its way onto Google Earth. The island does not exist.

Since the 1860's, the southern Indian state of Kerala has experienced rain that has been red, yellow, green, and black.

HISTORY

New Mexico was named almost 300 years before the country of Mexico by Spanish conquistadors.

In September 1968, during a protest outside Miss America, symbolic products were thrown in a bin including bras. A local reporter said the lines "Men burn draft cards and what next? Will women burn bras?" and the bra burning myth was born.

Officially, the United States Continental Congress declared independence from Britain on July 2, 1776. It took two days for congress to agree to a draft document which is why the document reads July 4 as that was the day the approved version was signed.

Gunslingers in the wild west tended to only keep five bullets in their guns instead of six. One chamber was kept empty as a safety measure.

Marie Antoinette never said, "Let them eat cake".
In fact, the quote would have referred to brioche,
a type of French bread, and the quote itself
comes from 'Rousseau's Confessions', written
when she was 14.

Napoleon was above average height for his time.

No Viking ever wore a horned helmet.

The legend of the 300 Spartans tends to omit the
7000 other Greek soldiers at the start of the
battle and the 700 that remained after the bulk of
the Greek army was sent home.

The iron maiden was an 18th century invention.

Magellan wasn't the first to circumnavigate the globe as he was killed halfway through the journey in the Philippines. Eighteen of the original 260 crewmen made it back but the real claim belongs to Magellan's slave, Enrique, who Magellan had seized in Malay in an earlier voyage. He escaped when Magellan died a few hundred miles from where he had been originally enslaved.

The population of the entire island of Ireland is still 2 million fewer than it was before the great famine in 1845.

Half of all humans who have ever lived have died from malaria.

Flyting is an ancient form of rap battles that took place among ancient Celtic and Viking men.

The Great Fire of London burned for 4 days in 1666 destroying 13,200 houses, 87 churches, St Paul's Cathedral and left at least 70,000 homeless. There were only six verified deaths.

George Washington was not the first president of the United States, only the first after the creation of the constitution. The post of president was held by 14 men before he was elected.

September, October, November, and December all have numeral prefixes of 7, 8, 9 and 10 because they used to be the 7th, 8th, 9th, and 10th months of the year.

During prohibition, Winston Churchill got a prescription from his doctor to show that he needed to drink alcohol when visiting the United States.

Britain planned to overthrow Lenin and replace the Bolsheviks with a military dictatorship.

Violet Constance Jessop was as a steward on the RMS Olympic on September 20, 1911, when it collided with the British warship HMS Hawke. In 1912 she was on its sister ship, Titanic on April 14, 1912, when it struck an iceberg. Four years later she was on HMS Britannic, the younger sister ship of Olympic and Titanic, when it sank after an explosion. She died aged eighty-three on dry land.

The year before John Wilkes Booth killed Abraham Lincoln, Booth's brother, Edwin, saved the life of Lincoln's son, Robert Todd, when the latter was about to fall onto train tracks in Washington, D.C.

Cleopatra was Greek.

The first man to die during the building of the Hoover Dam was J.G. Tierney, on December 20, 1922. The final man to die on the project, died seven years later, also on December 20. His name was Patrick W. Tierney, J.G. Tierney's son.

Oxford University was founded over three hundred years before the Aztec empire but is still eight years younger than the University of Bologna.

When Harvard was founded, Galileo was still alive.

When the Great Pyramid in Giza was built there was still a population of woolly mammoths on Earth.

The world's first set of written human rights were created by Cyrus the Great, King of Persia in the 6th century BC.

George Washington never lived in Washington, D.C.

The population of the Americas was 50 million when Columbus "discovered" it.

Kilts, bagpipes, haggis, whiskey, and tartan have one thing in common: They are not Scottish inventions.

No one really knows which way the thumb was supposed to go to indicate that a gladiator should be killed in Roman arenas.

Ribena was such an important source of vitamin C in the United Kingdom during World War II that two fake factories were built to confuse German bombers.

US President Lincoln's wife, Mary, was a drug addict due her use of over-the-counter drugs containing alcohol and opium.

The world's oldest wooden building is the Horyuji Temple near Nara in Japan. It was built around 700AD.

We will never know Einstein's last words because he said them in German to a nurse who didn't speak German.

The last emperor of China spent his final years as a street sweeper, a gardener and as a newspaper editor.

In Victorian Britain, brandy and oysters were considered a poor man's meal.

During the World War I Christmas truce of 1914 an English soldier got a haircut from a German soldier who used to be his hairdresser in London.

During World War II, Foyles bookshop in London, England, protected itself from bombs by covering its roof with copies of 'Mein Kampf.'

King Francis I of France hung the Mona Lisa in his bathroom.

French was an official language in Italy three years before it was the official language of France.

Rasputin had 7 children and his daughter, Maria, became a professional lion tamer.

In 1518 there was a dancing epidemic in Strasbourg in the Alsace. For three months people danced uncontrollably for up to six days, before collapsing and dying.

The US built a fort in 1816 to defend itself from Canada. Unfortunately, it was accidentally built in Canada itself, and it is called Fort Blunder.

Queen Victoria owned a bullet-proof umbrella.

Aldous Huxley and C.S. Lewis died on the same day President Kennedy was assassinated.

The Nazis were the first government in modern history to start an anti-smoking and tobacco movement.

In the 18th century, a group of pirates known as the Flying Gang, attacked ships by flying kites to hoist themselves up the sides of ships and then dropping down onto the decks.

During the 1850s and 1860s, engineers in Chicago solved the problem of the city lying in low-lying swampy ground by lifting streets, sidewalks, and brick buildings by between four and fourteen feet.

Tsutomu Yamaguchi was less than two miles from ground zero in Hiroshima for work when the first atomic bomb hit. He survived and the next day he made his way home to Nagasaki. Two days later while in a meeting the second atomic bomb exploded. He lived to be ninety-three.

The Nazis were working on producing a nuclear weapon.

The first native to greet the settlers at the Plymouth colony not only spoke English, but walked into their camp to say hello and ask if they had beer.

The oldest "your mom" joke was discovered etched onto a 3,500-year-old Babylonian tablet in Iraq in 1976.

Alarm clock production in the United States was stopped in 1942 to redirect resources to the war effort. Production was restarted in 1944, as too many workers missed their shifts when their alarm clock broke, and they could not purchase a new one.

We know that Antony and Cleopatra were buried together but despite being Egypt's most famous Queen, the tomb of Cleopatra has never been found.

The Han dynasty of China drilled for natural gas, transported it in pipelines and containers and burned it in stoves in 200 BC.

The world's oldest known boomerang was discovered in Poland in eastern Europe.

In ancient Egypt only the Pharoah and the Gods were allowed to eat marshmallows.

The longest war in recorded history lasted 335 years and 19 days. It was between the Netherlands and the Isles of Scilly, that are now part of the United Kingdom. There were no casualties, and the Dutch forgot about the conflict until a Scilly historian contacted them about it in 1985. A treaty was signed between them in 1986.

During the Dublin Whiskey Fire of 1897, 13 people died, not from the fire inhalation but from alcohol poisoning caused by the "rivers of whiskey" that filled the streets.

One of the pilgrims on the Mayflower, William Mullins, sailed with 139 pairs of shoes.

George Washington once called a ceasefire during the revolutionary war to allow the retrieval of a British General's terrier that had run on the battlefield.

During World War I, French soldiers were issued a daily ration of Camembert and red wine.

The oldest human hair was found in the fossilized feces of a hyena.

The world's first speeding ticket was issued in 1896 in the UK. The driver, Walter Arnold, was allegedly traveling at 8 miles per hour, four times the 2 miles per hour speed limit.

During the occupation of France in 1940, Citroen was forced to produce vehicles for the Nazis. They moved the fill line on their oil dipsticks lower, causing the trucks to seize under stress from low oil.

The most popular hat worn by men in the American wild west wasn't the Stetson or the ten-gallon hat but the bowler hat.

The ten-gallon hat got its name from the Spanish word "Galón," for braid.

The first person picked up by Vancouver's first Auto Ambulance was a man that the ambulance had run over on its first test drive.

Before electricity, people in many parts of the world would have two sleeps with the period in between filled with chores or people going out and visiting each other.

In 1994, the design for the new South African flag was sent to Nelson Mandela for approval. The colorful design was sent by fax so came out black and white. Somebody had to buy some coloring pencils and color in the flag.

The oldest known print advertisement dates from the year 1107 in China. It was for 'Jinan Liu's Fine Needle Shop'.

A medieval English recipe was found to cure MRSA, an infection characterized by a resistance to antibiotics. It consists of wine, garlic, leek, and ox gall standing in a brass vessel for nine days.

Werner Goldberg was the image of "The Ideal German Soldier" in 1939, used in recruitment posters and propaganda. Two years later he was discharged from the army because his father was Jewish.

Until 1956, French schools were permitted to serve students under 14 up to half a liter of wine, cider, or beer with a meal.

In 1962, the Philippines were considering renaming the country to "Malaysia" but before the senate had a chance to vote on it, the country now known as Malaysia officially adopted the name.

Zheng Yi Sao was a notorious female pirate who operated in the South China Sea in the early 19th century. She had a fleet of 300 ships and 40,000 crew members and retired with a pardon.

ENTERTAINMENT

Paul McCartney and John Lennon met at a church fete in Liverpool. One of the songs McCartney would later write was Eleanor Rigby which was a name he said he came up with as a combination of an actress's name and a store name. However, just yards from where the two met at that church fete is a gravestone that bears the name Eleanor Rigby.

The world's longest musical piece is the performance of the organ version of 'As Slow as Possible' currently being played in Halberstadt, Germany. Began in 2001 it's scheduled to be played for 639 years, ending in 2640.

On the 18th of April 1930, the BBC 20:45 news bulletin announced that. "There is no news". The rest of the 15-minute program was filled with piano music.

The producers of The Sopranos added a gun to the logo because HBO was worried viewers would think it was a show about music.

The blood in the shower scene in Psycho was watered down chocolate syrup.

Shaggy in Scooby-Doo has a proper name: Norville Rogers.

Keith Richards, co-founder of the Rolling Stones, was a choir boy at the coronation of Queen Elizabeth II.

The song "Mahna Mahna" made famous by The Muppets was originally created for a sex exploitation movie.

Keith Richards and Mick Jagger were neighbors and went to the same school for 11 years. They went their separate ways when both families moved but met again entirely by accident on a train platform seven years later.

The Beach Boys song "Never Learn Not to Love" was an altered version of "Cease to Exist", written by cult leader Charles Manson.

Italian singer Adriano Celentano released a song in Italy in 1972 full of gibberish made to sound like English words sung in an American accent. It was called Prisencolinensinainciusol which is also gibberish.

As a boy Roald Dahl, writer of Charlie and the Chocolate factory, attended a school that was sent chocolate by the local factory for the children to taste test.

Leo Fender, creator of the most iconic electric guitars in the world, couldn't play guitar.

Oscar Hammerstein is the only person named Oscar ever to win an Oscar.

The first winner of the Academy Award for Best Picture in 1927, Wings, had nudity and the first kiss between two men.

Barry Manilow's hit song "I write the songs" wasn't written by Barry Manilow.

Using a car door for cover during a gun fight is a bad idea as it's unlikely to give you much protection.

James Bond is famous for his Martinis in the movies but in the original books it's Scotch and soda that he prefers.

Elvis was a natural blond.

The Villains in the movies Psycho, Silence of the Lambs and The Texas Chainsaw Massacre are all based on the same man, Edward Gein of Wisconsin, USA.

Chewbacca was named after the Russian for dog, 'sobaka'.

Simpsons creator Matt Groening's mother was called Marge Wiggum.

Shirley Temple always had exactly 56 curls in her hair.

The mechanical shark in JAWS was called Bruce.

Psycho was the first major US movie to feature a flushing toilet.

Horror movies are the only genre of movie in which more women appear than men.

The term 'slapstick' comes from 16th century Italian comedy where a stick was used to make a slapping noise so the actor would not need to be hit.

One of singer and musician Prince's sisters claims his favorite color was orange, not purple.

Steve Irwin owned a tortoise that was once owned by English naturalist Charles Darwin.

Mickey Mouse has a sister named Amelia Fieldmouse.

The Human Torch was the first Marvel superhero ever created but was about an android that could control fire, not Johnny Storm of the Fantastic Four.

France gave Fifty Shades of Grey a rating of "12", meaning that only children under the age of twelve are prohibited from seeing it.

E.T., Gremlins and Poltergeist all came from one script written for another movie entirely.

The first in-flight movie was shown in 1925. It was a silent film and appeared on a Deutsche Lufthansa flight.

One of the Bond girls in the James Bond movie, For Your Eyes Only, is transgender.

Billie Jean by Michael Jackson was the first video to air on MTV by a black artist.

Internationally, Baywatch is the most popular television show in history.

Actor James Doohan, best known for playing "Scotty" on Star Trek, lost the middle finger on his right hand leading Canadian troops up Juno Beach on D-Day.

Captain Kirk never said, "Beam me up, Scotty."

In the movie, Casablanca, Rick never says, "Play it again, Sam."

The Japanese kana code you see in the beginning of the Matrix movie came from a book of sushi recipes.

Dolly Parton and Charlie Chaplin both entered look-a-like contests of themselves, and they both lost.

Daytime dramas are called Soap Operas because they were originally used to advertise soap powder. In America in the early days of television, advertisers would write stories about the use of their soap powder.

Sean Connery turned down the roles of Gandalf in Lord of the Rings, John Hammond in Jurassic Park, Morpheus and The Architect in The Matrix, Dumbledore in Harry Potter, Deckard in Blade Runner and Simon Gruber in Die Hard with a Vengeance.

Gene Roddenberry wrote lyrics to the Star Trek theme tune in order to claim half the royalties.

The Hulk was supposed to be grey but problems with the printing press meant the gray was never consistent, so they changed him to green.

There is a thirty-mile zone around Los Angeles where filming is considerably cheaper due to union rules. As a result, many American TV shows and movie sets will seem familiar because they are all filmed inside this zone.

Tom and Jerry were originally named Jasper and Jinx.

Originally, Superman could leap tall buildings in a single bound, but he wasn't able to fly.

David Bowie would often carry a Greek newspaper while traveling in New York, to give the impression that he was a Greek man who resembled him.

Cameron Diaz bought marijuana from Snoop Dogg while the two were in High School together.

Lisa Kudrow published an academic paper in neurology the same year that Friends debuted on TV.

Natalie Portman graduated from Harvard in 2003 with a B.A. in psychology. She missed the premiere of The Phantom Menace so she could study for her high school exams and was a co-author on two scientific papers.

Bryan Keith "Dexter" Holland, the singer, guitarist, and songwriter for the punk rock band The Offspring has a master's degree and PHD in microbiology.

Sir Alec Guinness hated his role as Obi-Wan Kenobi.

The red-carpet culture dates to ancient Greece where the "Crimson path" was a luxury fit only for the gods.

You cannot shoot a hat off a person's head; the bullet will not transfer enough energy.

In 1957 Little Richard saw a bright red fireball flying across the sky, which he took as "sign from God" to repent from performing secular music and his wild lifestyle. The fireball was the launch of the first artificial Earth satellite Sputnik 1.

There is no drug proven to make someone tell the truth. Sodium pentothal, the drug referred to in some movies, simply lowers inhibitions.

China banned Back to the Future because of its irresponsible use of time travel for entertainment.

The first charity single was for veterans of the Battle of Balaklava in 1890. It was 'Bugle Call of the Light Brigade' by Martin Lanfried, who played the same call he played for the infamous Charge of the Light Brigade.

According to her final wish, Elizabeth Taylor arrived late for her own funeral.

Actor Bill Murray doesn't use an agent or manager. He uses a toll-free phone number instead, that film makers can use to make their pitch.

Yoda and Miss Piggy were voiced by the same person.

The original Kermit the Frog was made from the green coat owned by the mother of his creator, Jim Henson.

The first bond movie and the first Beatles single were released on the same day.

King Charles III of Great Britain is a long-standing member of The Magic Circle.

Actress Hedy Lamarr was involved in the invention of frequency-hopping technology that formed the basis for Wi-Fi, Bluetooth, and GPS.

A recently discovered natural compound that is effective at killing fungi has been named Keanumycin, after Keanu Reeves, because he is also deadly in the roles he plays.

Britain's first animated feature film, 'Animal Farm' in 1954, was funded by the CIA.

On the television series Game of Thrones, a decapitated prosthetic head of former President George W. Bush was shown on a spike.

David Bowie first appeared on television aged 17, as the founder of the Society for the Prevention of Cruelty to Long-Haired Men.

When a Hollywood movie has more than one writer, an "&" indicates that the screenwriters collaborated on the script. An "and" means they worked independently on separate drafts.

Mozart had a sister, Maria Anna, who was also an extremely talented child prodigy in music and considered to be one of the most talented keyboard players of her time. Due to the rules of society at the time, she was prevented from performing as an adult.

On 24 January 1975, a concert was performed by Keith Jarrett at the Opera House in Cologne, Germany. The concert, organized by an 18-year-old promoter, was beset by problems including not being allowed to start until 11:30pm, the wrong piano being delivered and in such poor condition it required hours of tuning, Jarrett requiring a brace for severe back pain and a dinner mix-up that meant had to play without eating. Despite all of that, a recording of the concert, released as a double-vinyl album later that year, became the best-selling solo album in jazz history and the best-selling piano album of the year with sales of over 4 million.

LAW & ORDER

At least twenty individual feet have been found on the shores of the Salish Sea in north America.

An unidentified man hijacked Northwest Orient Airlines Flight 305 in the United States November 24, 1971. He escaped capture by opening the aft door of the plane and jumping out mid-flight wearing a parachute. He was never identified or apprehended.

On December 4, 2003, lawyer Jonathan Luna was found dead, face down in a creek. Despite being stabbed 36 times with his own pocketknife, he had drowned to death. No suspects or motive for murder were determined. The local authorities deemed it to be homicide, but the FBI called it a suicide.

Until 2006 it was illegal to worship Greek gods in Greece.

In 1985 a murder suspect in Texas, USA, was convicted after the broken-off leg of a grasshopper caught on his trousers turned out to be a perfect match for an insect found near the victim's body.

In the 1980s, Pablo Escobar's Medellin Cartel spent more than $2,500 a month on rubber bands, just to hold all their cash.

Under the US constitution, an accused has a right to a jury composed of people from the state where a crime was committed and from the federal district where it was committed. Fifty square miles of Yellowstone National Park are both in Idaho and the District of Wyoming, but nobody lives in the Idaho part of the park so a jury could never be formed and theoretically, a crime could be committed there, and no one could be tried for it.

On Oct. 31, 1969, Raffaele Minichiello hijacked TWA Flight 85 from Baltimore to San Francisco because he felt he was owed $200 pay by the army. He had the plane diverted to his native Italy where he became a heartthrob and media sensation. As a result, the Italian government refused to extradite him and charged him only with weapons possession for which he served 18 months.

Prison inmate James Washington suffered a heart attack in 2009 and believed he was about to die. In an effort to clear his conscience, while being escorted to a hospital, he turned to a guard and confessed to the murder of a woman. He survived the heart attack and was later convicted of the woman's murder by his own confession.

A 12-year-old girl kidnapped in south-west Ethiopia in June 2005 was rescued when three lions chased her kidnappers off and guarded the girl until police arrived.

Sir Arthur Conan Doyle, writer of the Sherlock Holmes stories, was involved in solving two real criminal cases.

In 2009 Irish police were looking for a Polish man called Prawo Jazdy who had committed over 50 driving offenses across the country. Only later did they discover that prawo jazdy means driving license in the Polish.

Between 1993 and 2009 a serial killer seemed to be at large across Europe, with the same DNA from a female, believed to be of East European origin, discovered at forty different crime scenes in Austria, France, and Germany. The criminal was dubbed the "Phantom of Heilbronn". Only in 2009 did investigators realize that the DNA belonged to a woman who worked in the cotton swab factory that made the DNA test kits who had contaminated the swabs with her own DNA.

On 25 November 2012 New York city experienced its first day since the 1960's where there were no recorded murders, manslaughter, or violent crime.

In 2017, Police in Frankfurt, Germany found a car belonging to a 76-year-old man who had forgotten where he parked it. Twenty years earlier.

20% of all the prisoners in the world are in prison in the United States.

In Quitman, Georgia in the United States, chickens are not allowed to cross the road.

Snake charming is illegal in India.

Krystian Bala, a Polish author, wrote a crime novel in 2003 which quickly became a bestseller. It gripped the nation and received a lot of publicity. Police found many of the details about the murder in the novel strangely similar to an unsolved case regarding the torture and murder of Darusz Janiszewski. Digging deeper they found that Krystian had known the victim, was the last person to have seen him alive and had sold Janiszewski's mobile phone.

Several countries in the Caribbean including Barbados, Jamaica, Grenada, Dominica, St. Lucia, and St. Vincent ban the wearing of camouflage patterned clothes by civilians.

On June 9, 2011, 59-year-old James Verone robbed a bank in North Carolina, USA, demanding just $1 in order to be sent to prison so that he could receive medical treatment as he couldn't afford medical insurance.

Landlords are allowed to place a curfew on flushing toilets after 10:00 PM in Switzerland.

Kwame Nkrumah, Ghana's first president, ran and won his campaign from prison.

In June 2008, Finnish police found a dead mosquito inside an abandoned car that had been reported stolen. The mosquito was sent for analysis, and the DNA in the blood it had ingested from its last meal was used to identify the car thief.

In 2019, Brazilian police seized a parrot who had been taught to alert criminals to police operations by shouting: "Mum, the police!".

In 1974, police in Oakland, USA, spent two hours trying to convince a mentally disturbed gunman holed up in his apartment to surrender, only to discover that he was standing next to them pretending to help.

Australia's first police force was made entirely out of the best-behaved criminals.

André Stander, a South African police officer, robbed almost 30 banks. Sometimes he would carry out a crime during his lunch break and then return to the scene as an investigating officer.

Al Capone's older brother, James Vincenzo Capone, worked in law enforcement.

From 1911 until 1966, it was illegal to grow blackcurrants in the United States and continued to be illegal in most states until 2003.

Jack Daniel's whiskey is produced in a dry county where alcohol cannot be sold anywhere.

In November 2017, undercover officers from Detroit's 11th district arrived at a suspected drug house posing as buyers. When the presence of drugs was confirmed, more officers stormed the property. Unfortunately, the dealers were also undercover officers from Detroit's 12th district. The ensuing fight ended with one policeman in hospital.

Japanese police fire paintballs at fleeing vehicles so that other police vehicles can identify them later if they get away. The paint is Bright orange and difficult to remove.

In Canada, until 2018, it was illegal to pretend to be a witch but completely legal to practice witchcraft.

Henryk Siwiak was shot on September 11, 2001, in New York City. His death is the only homicide recorded on that date as New York does not include the deaths from the terror attacks in its official crime statistics.

Leaving the United States with more than $5.00 in five-cent and one-cent coins is a crime that could result in a jail sentence of five years.

Escaping from Alcatraz using a raft made from rain ponchos is feasible.

Riot control agents such as pepper spray are used regularly by the police on civilian protestors but because they are listed officially as chemical weapons, they are forbidden in warfare.

An episode of Curb Your Enthusiasm cleared a man of murder. After five months in jail, Juan Catalan was released when footage of a Dodgers game cut from the show caught Catalan in the background, providing him with an alibi. In the footage, Catalan was eating a hot dog.

Mob boss Vincent Gigante used to walk around New York in a bathrobe to convince the police he was insane.

The first crime prosecuted using fingerprint evidence was the theft of billiard balls.

In Mexico, non-violent attempts to escape prison
are not illegal and will not be punished.

BIOLOGY, MEDICINE, AND HEALTH

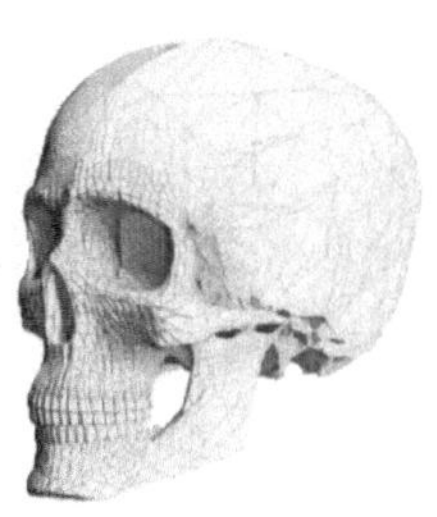

A single sperm carries 37.5MB worth of data.

When your mother was born, she was already carrying the egg that would become you.

Humans have four nostrils.

Your veins appear to be blue because blue light does not penetrate human tissue as deeply as red light.

Semi-identical twins are twins born when two sperms fertilize one egg. The twins will share identical chromosomes from the mother but only 50% of the fathers.

Our sense of smell and taste decreases between 20% and 50% at high altitudes.

Humans shed an average of 40 pounds (18.1 kilograms) of skin in their lifetime.

Much like the eyes can be tricked by optical illusions, the ears can be tricked by aural illusions.

Fingernails and hair do not keep growing after death. They only appear to do so because the because the skin around them has retracted.

Vitamin C does not prevent colds.

A broken heart is a real physical ailment. It is called stress-induced cardiomyopathy.

Science does not really know why we sleep.

There are no specific areas on your tongue for different tastes. The ability to taste sweet, salty, sour, and bitter isn't split to different parts of the tongue.

You don't need to drink eight glasses of water a day.

We do not use just 10% of our brains. In fact, most of the brain is active almost all the time.

There is no link between the amount of sugar a child consumes and the level of hyper-activity they display.

The uniform dark grey background that many people report seeing when you open your eyes in a pitch-black room is called Eigengrau or brain gray.

Twins can have two different fathers.

The placebo effect still works up to 60% of the time even when people are told it's a placebo at the outset.

Human brains are smaller than they were 20,000 years ago.

No one knows why we yawn.

Almost all Koreans do not have the gene for smelly armpits.

Humans have at least nine senses.

Humans are the only animals that blush.

The human nose can detect over one trillion different scents.

Wounds sustained during the day heal almost twice as fast as wounds sustained at night.

High-risk patients with heart failure and cardiac arrest hospitalized in teaching hospitals have up to 10% lower 30-day mortality when admitted during dates of national cardiology meetings when senior physicians are away.

Your eardrums move when you move your eyeballs. No one knows why.

There is a disease called Cotard's Syndrome that makes people believe they are dead.

The human eye can detect a single photon.

There is little evidence that flossing works.

Women who take birth control blink 32% more than women who do not take birth control. The cause is still unknown.

Hispanics in the United States live longer lives than non-Hispanic White Americans despite having lower average income and education. Researchers have not been able to find out exactly why.

It is impossible to walk in a straight line if your eyes are closed.

Cracking your knuckles will not give you arthritis or any other kind of problems with your joints.

You cannot lick your own elbow.

All the muscles in the human body can only pull not push. Sticking your tongue out requires muscles pulling in different directions to pull your tongue forward.

Your fingers don't wrinkle in water because the skin is absorbing water but because blood vessels are constricting. Scientists are not sure why it happens.

It is not dangerous to wake up a person who is sleepwalking.

Viagra can make your vision blue.

Red placebos are more effective pain relievers than placebos in any other color.

Humans use two hundred muscles with every step.

Paracetamol, otherwise known as acetaminophen and sold under brand names like Tylenol and Panadol, relieves fevers and pain. But scientists do not really know how.

Six minutes after consuming an amount of alcohol equivalent to three glasses of beer or two glasses of wine, human brain cells began to react.

WORLD FACTS

There are twelve fake houses in Paris, France and two in London, England. They hide ventilations shafts, electrical transformers and, in London, an open-air section of the London Underground where locomotives would vent off steam in the 1800's.

Five provinces of China would be in the top twenty most populous countries in the world.

There is only one stop sign in Paris, France and it's located at the end of a company's drive.

Until 2015, the Swiss Airforce was only able to intercept illegal flights in its airspace during office hours.

An estimated 90% of the population of the Earth lives in the Northern Hemisphere.

If the entire world lived in as dense a population as New York city, everyone would fit in the state of Texas in the US.

The lost property office at Dublin airport has an unclaimed headstone that carries the words: 'You will always be remembered, never forgotten.'

4% of Canadians live south of Seattle, a city that is in the United States.

Saudi Arabia has to buy sand and camels from Australia.

71% of the world owns 3% of global wealth, The next 21% own a further 12% and then next 7% own 40% of the wealth. The wealthiest 1% own the remaining 45%.

1 in 10 of all people in Asia are descended from Genghis Khan according to a study of Y-chromosomes in men in countries that were part of the Mongol Empire.

54 million people alive right now in the world will be dead within 12 months.

1 in 10 European children are conceived on an Ikea bed.

The heads on Easter Island have bodies.

25% of couples in the United States sleep in separate beds.

People who don't have a name for a color can't see it. The Himba tribe of Namibia use the same word for green and blue so cannot distinguish a blue from a green. However, they can see shades of green that English speakers have trouble seeing.

The voodoo doll can be traced back to the European poppet, Egyptian priests and ancient Greece. But it is not part of the Voodoo religion.

In the United States, it is legal to own a kangaroo without having a permit in three states but in four states it is legal to own a tiger without a permit.

You can buy a room on some cruise ships and live there.

A 2012 study of maritime disasters found that the notion of 'women and children first' is a myth with the Titanic disaster being the only exception they could find.

The population of Bangladesh is 115% bigger than Russia while the nation is 115 times smaller.

The United States uses more electricity just for air-conditioning than the whole of Africa uses in total.

No one knows why the Finns called Finland Suomi.

After marriage, the amount of time a man spends doing chores on a weekly basis decreases significantly.

The entire state of Wyoming only has two escalators.

The arches at the base of the Eiffel Tower are just for decoration and serve no purpose.

People tend to find fewer insects smashed on the windscreens of their cars now compared to a decade or several decades ago. This is called the windshield phenomenon.

More than half the species on the planet are moving their habitat because of climate change.

Built sometime during the Inca period, Queshuachaca is the last surviving Inca grass rope bridge, and the locals rebuild it every summer.

Due to the size of the Vatican City State, embassies accredited to the Holy See are based on Italian territory, making The Embassy of Italy to the Holy See the only embassy in the world based in its home territory.

The United States is currently under 42 different national emergencies, one of which dates from 1979. This is because once declared it is indefinite unless it is terminated by the President or Congress.

The Limite Zero zip line crosses from Spain to Portugal, making it the only one in the world that crosses both a time-zone and a border.

The Japanese Daisugi technique has been used for 700 years in Japan and allows shoots from the base of a tree to be pruned so that the trunk stays straight and a harvest of straight logs to be gathered without needing to cut trees down.

PEOPLE

The Wright Brothers, John Glenn, and Neil Armstrong, the first men to fly, the first American in space and the first man on the Moon respectively, had one thing in common: They were all from the state of Ohio in the United States, along with another 22 astronauts including Jim "Houston we have a problem" Lovell.

Alan Eustace set the current world record for highest and longest-distance free fall jump in 2014 when he jumped from 135,898 feet (41.422 km).

Swimmer Lewis Pugh can Increase his body temperature to 38.4°C.

Human life expectancy has increased more in the last 50 years than in the previous 200,000 years of human existence.

Stephen Wiltshire is a British architectural artist and autistic savant that can draw an accurate detailed picture of a subject after looking at it just once. He drew a nineteen-foot-long drawing of 305sq miles of New York City after one twenty-minute helicopter ride.

Daniel Kish is blind man who uses echolocation by clicking his tongue to form a map of his surrounding area.

The closer to the equator a woman lives, the more likely she is to conceive a girl.

Dean Karnazescan can run without ever getting tired due to his exponentially high lactate threshold. He was able to run a Marathon in the south pole at -25°C for three consecutive nights before having to stop for sleep.

In 1999 while over North Carolina USA, both of Joan Murray's parachutes failed and she fell 14,500 feet. She landed on a mound of stinging red ants who stung her over 200 times. Those bites kept enough adrenalin in her system for her heart to keep beating long enough for her to be rescued and survive.

Serbian flight attendant Vesna Vulović set the record for the highest a person has fallen and survived without a parachute in 1972 when a bomb exploded on her plane at 33,333 feet.

A person will stay drier in the rain if they run rather than walk.

People who have had Botox can't frown and struggle to read difficult sentences.

Two identical twin brothers, James 'Jim' Lewis and James 'Jim' Springer were adopted by two separate families at birth. Both families named the new sons James but called them Jim. Before ever meeting, both men married women with the same first name, Linda. Both men got divorced and married a second time, both to a women called Betty. Both had dogs with the same name, Toy, and both had a brother called Larry. Both men had a son who they both called James Alan. Both men were heavy smokers who drove the same kind of car. One was a security guard while the other was a deputy sheriff. They finally met at the age of 39.

Nobody knows or can tell if we all see colors the same way.

In 1996 Indian civil engineer Chewang Norphel invented the artificial glacier and between 1996 and 2012 he built twelve in Northern India, ending years of water shortages in the area.

Dr Barry Marshall was convinced that H. Pylori bacteria causes stomach ulcers, but no one believed him. Since it was illegal to test his theory on humans, he drank the bacteria himself, developed ulcers within days, treated them with antibiotics and went on to win a Nobel prize.

Adults can judge the temperature of water simply from hearing it being poured.

In 2007 45-year-old Florida resident Michael Moylan, woke up with a severe headache and asked his wife to drive him to a hospital, where doctors found a bullet lodged behind his right ear. His wife had shot him while he slept.

Robert Chesebrough, the inventor of petroleum jelly ate a spoonful every day, claiming it had tremendous health benefits. He lived to be ninety-six.

William Phelps Eno, an American businessman, invented the stop sign, the pedestrian crossing, the roundabout, the one-way street, the taxi-stand, and pedestrian safety islands. He was known as the 'Father of traffic safety' but he never learned to drive a car.

One day every year, South Korea comes to a standstill for Suneung, an eight-hour national graduation test for high-school students. Businesses shut or open late, construction work halts, planes are grounded and military training ceases. Students running late for the test may be escorted to their testing site by police officers via motorcycle.

Hysterical strength is a phenomenon in which individuals exhibit superhuman strength at a level far beyond what is considered normal or possible. Many cases have been documented but the mechanism behind it is not understood.

Marie Curie is the only person to earn a Nobel prize in two different sciences.

The man who named the Panda (referring to the red panda) was the younger brother of the man who named the pterodactyl.

The first female and the first black self-made millionaire in America was known as Madam C.J. Walker but was born Sarah Breedlove. She was orphaned at the age of 7 and was the child of former slaves.

On December 30, 1952, a London double-decker bus found itself on London's famous Tower Bridge as it suddenly started opening. The driver, Albert Gunter, made the split-second decision to accelerate and jumped the bus across the gap created by the opening bridge.

Peoples in Southeast Asia build bridges by manipulating the roots of trees. These bridges can take more than one generation to complete and can last hundreds of years.

One of the inventors of the first mechanical artificial heart, Dr. Paul Winchell, was also the original voice of Tigger from Winnie the Pooh, Gargamel from the Smurfs and Dick Dastardly in Wacky Races.

FOOD & DRINK

Tea has more caffeine than coffee before the brewing process but tea leeches far less caffeine during brewing.

Erich von Wolf misplaced a decimal point when recording his research on the iron content of green vegetables, making the iron content in spinach ten times greater than it really is and spawning one of the longest lasting myths of the last century.

The name PEZ comes from the German word for peppermint, "PfeffErminZ" taking the P from the first letter, E from the middle and Z from the last letter to form the word PEZ.

Cappuccino' takes its name from the Capuchin friars as the colors of the espresso mixed with frothed milk were similar to the color of their robes.

Parmesan is the most stolen food stuff on the planet and the regional bank, Credito Emiliano will accept Parmesan as collateral for loans. They are estimated to hold over $200 million in cheese in their vaults. There have been three robberies at the bank, all targeting the cheese.

When Italian baker, Pietro Ferrero, realized he did not have enough chocolate due to rationing in World War II, he added the one thing his region had in abundance, hazelnuts. The "Pasta Gianduja" sold as a block in 1946 and the creamy Super Crema in 1951. In 1963 it was renamed Nutella.

Blackberries, mulberries, and raspberries are not berries, but bananas, pumpkins, avocados, and cucumbers are.

Tortilla chips can spontaneously combust.

Carrots farmed before the 16th century were dark purple. The Dutch developed the orange carrot in the 16th century and although there are tales that they were bred to honor William of Orange there is no evidence to prove it.

Peanuts, chestnuts, cashews, and almonds are not nuts.

William Morrison, one of the two inventors of machine spun cotton candy, was a dentist.

Chili con carne is not a Mexican dish. It was invented in Texas, in the United States.

In the 1830s, tomato ketchup was sold as a cure for diarrhea.

Several years before the monk Dom Pérignon began his experiments at the Benedictine Abbey at Hautvillers, Englishman, Christopher Merrett originally described the distinctive 'méthode champenoise', a process of making sparkling wine by adding sugar.

Synsepalum dulcificum, or Miracle fruit, is a plant that grows in tropical Africa. It produces a berry that when eaten causes all sour foods to taste sweet for about 30 minutes.

Kopi luwak or civet coffee is one of the most expensive coffees in the world. It is produced from coffee beans which have been partially digested by the Indonesian palm civet and then excreted.

The name avocado derives from the Nahuatl word 'ahuacatl', which means testicle.

Cooling pasta lowers the calories your body digests and reheating it reduces the rise in blood sugar glucose levels by 50% after eating it.

Recent archaeological discoveries have shown that frogs legs were eaten in Britain 7000 years before the French started eating them.

There are more than one thousand types of bananas. Humans eat just one in its raw state. It used to be two, but one became extinct in 1965.

The banana we do eat is also technically extinct. Known as Cavendish, it is a hybrid of two other plant species. It has no seeds and has only been able to reproduce when cloned with the aid of farmers, who remove and transplant part of the plant's stem.

Bananas are radioactive because of their high levels of potassium, and pineapples contain arsenic.

Corn, avocado, cucumbers, peas, beans, and peppers are botanically fruit like tomatoes. In the United States, the Supreme Court ruled that tomatoes are vegetables.

Regular eating of carrots can turn your skin orange.

Eating grapefruit can alter the effects of 43 different kinds of medications.

Blowing out the candles on a cake increases the number of bacteria on it by 1400%.

There is chocolate bar made by Cadbury called a Flake. Its manufacturing process means when exposed to heat it won't melt.

Avocados, almonds, onions, and cucumbers are not vegan because of the use of migratory bees, otherwise known as slave bees, that are shipped from farm to farm to pollinate vast quantities of plants.

The Guinness Beer company's brewery in Dublin, Ireland was originally leased in 1759 for 9,000 years.

When John Harvey Kellogg invented corn flakes in 1894 it was deliberately made bland. As a Seventh-day Adventist, he believed bland food dulled the passions and reduced the desire for sexual activity.

M&Ms are named after their creators: Mars and Murrie.

One of the inventors of M&M's, Forrest Mars, was allergic to peanuts.

M&M's were the first chocolate in space.

After iodine was added to salt in 1924 the average American's IQ jumped by 15%.

Black apples are real and are Called Black Diamond apples. They are found in Tibet and are from the Hua Niu family of apples, also known as Chinese Red Delicious.

Almonds are part of the peach family.

Humans are the only animal that enjoys spicy foods. Tree shrews are known to seek out chillis, but they are not as sensitive to capsaicin so do not feel the hot effect.

Customers in a bookstore were 3 times more likely to peruse romantic books if the store smelt of chocolate, and 5 times more likely to buy them.

The man who designed the Pringles can, Fred Bauer, had his ashes buried in one.

Charred animal bones are used to give sugar its white color.

Figs' unique method of pollination involves a female fig wasp tunnelling into the center of the fig, laying its eggs and dying. The offspring hatch and take the pollen with them when they leave the fig.

Bird's nest soup, an expensive delicacy, is made from the partially dissolved nest of a swiftlet, a small bird native to Southeast Asia that builds their nests out of their sticky saliva on cave walls and cliff sides, where they raise their young.

Potatoes were the first food planted in space.

Beavers have an anal sac that produces castoreum, which is used in food and beverages as a substitute for vanilla flavoring.

Fruit salad trees grow different fruits on the same tree. These are called multi-grafted trees and they can grow up to six types of fruit at a time.

Brown sugar and white sugar are the same thing. The only difference is that in brown sugar some of the molasses lost during the refining process gets added back.

Honey never goes bad if stored properly.

The Australian billygoat plum, also known as the Kakadu plum contains 50 to 100 times more vitamin C than an orange.

Eating ice cream for breakfast can increase mental alertness.

The fish Sarpa salpa (known as the dreamfish) is a hallucinogenic when eaten.

The Quaker Oats company isn't run by Quakers nor was it started by them.

Eating only wild rabbit can be deadly due to protein poisoning.

Eating poppy seeds can lead to a positive drug test for opioids.

Pepperoni was invented in New York city.

The human body can't digest swallowed chewing gum, but it doesn't stay in your system for years. It will just pass through intact.

There is an official international standard for making the tea correctly (ISO 3103).

There is a delicacy that exists in Inuit culture called Urumiit, which is the feces of the ptarmigan bird.

MILITARY, POLITICS & GOVERNMENT

The US Civil War started in Bull Run in 1861 near Manassas, Virginia. Confederate General Beauregard took the home of one Wilmer McLean as his HQ. So, Mclean moved to Appomattox, Virginia. But four years later Mclean's new home was used to end the war when General Lee officially surrendered to General Grant in Mclean's parlor.

Samuel Hinkley of Cape Cod, who died in 1662 is an ancestor of both former US Presidents Bush and former US President Barak Obama.

When the tank was invented, it was officially called the "Landship". Tank was the code word for it.

The F-117 fighter uses aerodynamics discovered during research into how bumblebees fly.

The VIIC, an advanced class of German submarine during WWII was fitted with a state-of-the-art toilet system that was complicated to use. On 4 April 1945, the captain of U-1206 failed to work the flush mechanism correctly. Which caused the cabin to start flooding, which caused the seawater to leak into the battery compartment which caused the release of lethal amounts of chlorine gas. Left with no option the submarine had to surface where it was spotted by British Air Force patrols which lead to the boat being scuttled leading to four crew members drowning.

The last country invaded by Scotland was Panama.

Britain invented the concentration camp.

Canada has a Strategic Maple Syrup Reserve.

American tank crews have a superstition that will not allow them to eat apricots, allow apricots on board or within a one-mile radius of their tank or even say the word 'apricot'. The superstition started in WWII after people noticed that tanks carrying apricots broke down.

80% of United States elections are won by the taller candidate.

The US Department of Defense owns nearly thirty million acres of land worldwide with over seven hundred and thirty bases outside the US.

When worn on deployment, US Flag patches on uniforms are infrared so soldiers can be identified as friendly by others looking through night vision goggles.

During World War I, the British army converted the passenger ship RMS Carmania into a battleship. To avoid enemy fire, it was disguised to look like the German ship SMS Trafalgar. In 1914, the RMS Carmania sank a German ship off the coast of Brazil. The sunken ship was the SMS Trafalgar, which had been disguised to look like the British RMS Carmania.

The first armored car used by a US President was a Cadillac once owned by Al Capone.

At the start of Operation Good Hope, US forces were supposed to land on the beaches of Mogadishu under the cover of darkness. Instead, they were met by CNN who was covering the landing live on television.

The United States government has an official plan for a zombie apocalypse.

During the Austro-Prussian War, Liechtenstein had an army of 80 men. During the conflict no men were injured or killed, and they returned home with 81 men because they'd made an Italian friend along the way.

If you have served in the military, regardless of the branch of service, regardless of where you were deployed, and regardless of whether you served during a time of peace or a time of war, you are at a 60% greater risk of dying from ALS (motor neuron disease) and nobody knows why.

The US Government spent 20 years and $20m on an experimental project to test and train telepaths for military use. It was called the Stargate Project and closed in 1995.

President Kennedy's brain went missing after his autopsy and has never been found.

The Canadian government tried using a special machine in the 1950s and 1960s to identify and eliminate all gay men from the civil service, the Royal Canadian Mounted Police, and military.

The world's richest and most powerful men have an annual retreat in Bohemian Grove in Monte Rio, California in the US.

The sinking of the RMS Lusitania on 7 May 1915 was a major contributing factor to American entry into the First World War as all blame was laid on Germany for sinking a civilian ship. In 2008 was it revealed that it was carrying weaponry and ammunition for the British.

The world's oldest continuous government is the San Marino government, which was established in 301 AD.

Carrots don't help you see better at night. The myth is based on British disinformation posters in World War II trying to hide the invention of radar.

In 1939 the United States army was smaller than the armies of Portugal and Romania with 187,893 active-duty soldiers. By 1945 the army had nearly 8.3 million active-duty soldiers.

The United States's military spending is greater than the next nine countries combined. It has more ships than the next thirteen largest navies combined and more aircraft than the next eleven combined.

Between 1864 and 1870 Paraguay fought a war against Brazil, Uruguay, and Argentina. 90% of its male population were killed.

The shortest war in history was between Great Britain and Zanzibar. The war started on August 27, 1896. Zanzibar surrendered after just 38 minutes.

Before WWII, the United States Navy trained on the assumption that its next war would be against the British Empire. The plan was called the Atlantic Strategic War Plan.

Switzerland operates under a federal parliamentary democratic republic, with a unique system of direct democracy that allows citizens to propose and vote on laws.

Braille began as a military code called "night writing." Developed by the French army in 1819 to communicate in silence in darkness.

The first president of Vietnam, Ho Chi Minh, spent years travelling the world. He once worked as a cook in a hotel in Boston.

In 1996, Russia launched a Mars Rover called "Mars 96". It crashed back to earth after 2 days, containing 200 grams of plutonium-238 fuel which would have survived the impact. Nobody ever bothered to look for it, and it's believed to just be lying around the Andes mountains.

The US invaded Guatemala in 1954 and deposed democratically elected President Jacobo Árbenz Guzmán for the benefit of an American fruit company.

Because of the Electoral College, a presidential candidate can win with only 23% of the popular vote in the United States.

During the attack on Pearl Harbor, only 5 American pilots managed to get into the air against 353 Japanese planes. The first two were George Welch and Kenneth Taylor. They shot down six enemies. They were denied the Medal of Honor because they didn't have permission to take off from their commanding officer.

The US military was already using UAV drone technology in WWII. The primary manufacturer at that time, the Radioplane Company, had a drone assembler working for them named Norma Jeane Dougherty, who eventually changed her name to Marilyn Monroe.

Mitsuo Fuchida, the Japanese captain that led the attack on Pearl Harbor, later became a Christian and had a green card allowing permanent residence in the United States.

After the attack on Pearl Harbor, Canada declared war on Japan before the United States did.

Lenin spoke English with an Irish accent.

All the palm trees in Los Angeles are the result of a 1930s job creation scheme.

The oldest object in the British crown jewels is a spoon.

Until 1971 the US Postmaster General was last in line of succession to the presidency.

The earliest re-enactments of the American civil war took place before the American civil war ended.

Some police stations in China use guard geese instead of using guard dogs.

The oldest alliance in the world is between Britain and Portugal. It has been going since 1373.

United States civil defense guidelines advise against using hair conditioner after a nuclear strike.

The battle of Waterloo did not happen at Waterloo.

Napoleon was so popular in Britain after the battle of Waterloo, the authorities would not allow him to be brought into the country as a prisoner out of fear that he would cause an uprising so instead kept him on a ship offshore.

President Lyndon B. Johnson owned an Amphibious car, the Amphicar, and used it to scare guests by driving them into his lake screaming about brake failure.

On October 14, 1912, former United States President Theodore Roosevelt was shot in Milwaukee, Wisconsin. The bullet lodged in his chest after penetrating his steel eyeglass case and passing through 50 pages of a single-folded copy of the three-hour speech he was to give that he kept in his jacket. He went on to give the speech before going to hospital but cut it down to 84 minutes.

If you were listening to the radio in Vietnam in April 1975, you might have heard a surprising song: Bing Crosby's "White Christmas." It was the secret signal for Americans to evacuate the country.

In 1974 North Korea ordered 1,000 Volvo cars from Sweden. Although the cars were delivered, North Korea never paid the invoice on the cars.

In May 2021, American paratroopers with the 173rd Airborne Brigade mistakenly raided a working olive oil factory in Bulgaria as part of a large-scale NATO exercises.

In 1922 Rebecca Felton became the first woman to serve in the United States Senate and the last member of Congress to be a slave owner. As a stand-in senator she only served for one day.

In 2012 a scientific study predicted a 39-inch rise in sea level along the North Carolina coast over the next century. In response, North Carolina lawmakers passed a law banning the use of scientific predictions of sea level rise when considering new developments along the coast.

In the early 20th century, the German parliament had an official debate over which of two typefaces was more German.

In 1956, a weapons malfunction on an F11 Tiger aircraft caused it to shoot its own tail section, making it the only known military aircraft to have shot itself down.

Rosalynn Carter, first lady and wife of President Jimmy Carter was delivered by Lillian Gordy Carter, who was a registered nurse and midwife and Jimmy Carter's mother.

On 23 February 2008, Spirit of Kansas, a B-2 Spirit stealth bomber of the US Air Force, crashed on the runway moments after takeoff from Andersen Air Force Base in Guam. The aircraft was destroyed and at a cost of $1.4 billion, is the most expensive aircraft crash in history.

In March 1958, a B-47 plane headed to the United Kingdom from the United States accidentally released an atomic bomb, bigger than the bomb dropped on Nagasaki, while flying over South Carolina. The bomb lacked a fissile nuclear core so there was no nuclear detonation, but its conventional explosives injured six people.

SPORT & LEISURE

While over eleven thousand people have climbed Mount Everest, less than 1000 have reached the summit of K2, the world's second-highest mountain.

Between 1912 and 1948, art competitions were a part of the Olympics. Medals were awarded for architecture, music, painting, and sculpture.

The sum of all the numbers on a roulette wheel is 666.

Third man syndrome is an often-reported sensation that there was unseen presence during traumatic experiences. It is often reported by mountain climbers and has been reported by well-known adventurers and explorers including Ernest Shackelton in his expedition to the Antarctic.

Soccer is a word that originates in Britain not the United States. The sport was formally called Association Football and "assoc-er" became a slang word for the sport as it was common at the time to add -er to the end of nicknames. Rugby football was called "rugger". It remained soccer in the United States because football already referred to American Football.

The state sport of Alabama is figure skating, Pack burro racing in Colorado and jousting in Maryland.

A pack of cards randomly shuffled will never have been shuffled in the same way before and never will again.

Olympic gold medals are made of silver.

There is a far higher mortality rate among steeplechase medalists than in other athletics events and no one is sure why.

Despite running about three hours, actual playing time in a Major League Baseball game is under 18 minutes.

The earliest evidence of sport is in cave paintings in Mongolia dating back to 7000BC showing crowds watching a wrestling match, but some argue that paintings in the Lascaux caves in France depict wrestling and sprinting around 15,000 years ago.

A marathon race is 26 miles and 385 yards long. The final 385 yards were added in the 1908 London Olympics so that the runners would finish in front of the Royal family's viewing box in the main stadium.

The Men's 3000 Meters Steeplechase event at the 1932 Summer Olympics was 3460 meters. Due to an error in lap counting, the runners did an extra lap of the track.

Recently uncovered historical evidence hints that baseball was an English invention, and that the game's most direct antecedent is the English game of stoolball. The first recorded game of "Bass-Ball" took place in 1749 in Surrey, England, and featured the Prince of Wales as a player.

In 1873, Billiards became the first sport to have a world championship competition.

Pinball was illegal in Oakland, California until 2014.

Only one NFL player has died on the field. Chuck Hughes died of a heart attack in a game in 1971.

San Marino has only ever won three medals at the Summer Olympics but that still makes them the most successful country ever when measured by per head of population.

The last left-handed catcher to play in a Major League Baseball game was Benny Distefano who played for the Pittsburgh Pirates in 1989.

In June 1923, jockey Frank Hayes won a race at Belmont Racetrack despite having had a heart attack and dying mid-race. Since he stayed in the saddle, he was still officially the winner and is the only jockey in history to win a race posthumously.

The longest professional tennis match in history
was played at the 2010 Wimbledon
Championships between American John Isner
and Frenchman Nicolas Mahut. The match lasted
a total of 11 hours and 5 minutes over three days.
Recent rule changes mean this record is unlikely
to ever be beaten.

The highest recorded score in a game of
professional soccer where one of the teams was
not intentionally trying to lose is 36-0, which
occurred in a game between Arbroath and Bon
Accord in 1885. In modern times, the record
goes to Australia's 31-0 victory over American
Samoa in 2001.

James Fixx, credited with helping start America's
fitness revolution by popularizing the sport of
running, died from a heart attack while running at
the age of 52.

On August 17ᵗʰ, 1957, a foul ball hit during a baseball game hit Alice Roth in the face, breaking her nose. After receiving treatment, she was carried away on a stretcher and play resumed. The next ball was a foul ball and struck Roth, while still on the stretcher, on the leg breaking a bone in her knee.

The 26ᵗʰ President of the United States, Theodore Roosevelt, regularly had sparring sessions in the White House including taking on professional boxers. He ended up with a detached retina in one eye.

20,000-year-old fossilized human footprints discovered in Australia in 2003 indicate that one of them were made by a man running at 23 miles per hour (37 kph), the speed of a modern Olympic sprinter, while barefoot, in sand.

When he was 26, Pete Maravich said "I don't want to play 10 years in the NBA and die of a heart attack at age 40" in an interview. He went on to play 10 years in the NBA and died of a heart attack at age 40.

There is a Native American tribe of ultra-runners known as the Tarahumara. They can run 200 miles non-stop, and play running games that go on for up to 2 days without breaks.

The longest recorded rally in a professional tennis event was at the 1984 Virginia Slims tournament in Virginia where Vicki Nelson and Jean Hepner played out a 29 minute, 643 shot rally. In contrast, the shortest entire match in the modern era was when Francisco Clavet defeated Jiang Shan in 25 minutes.

Panama hats come from Ecuador, not Panama.

Adolf Hitler didn't snub Jesse Owens at the 1936 Olympics. He only congratulated German athletes on the first day and was told he must congratulate all or none. Hitler chose none.

Cleveland Indians pitcher Ray Caldwell was struck by lightning in the middle of the ninth inning in a game against the Philadelphia Athletics in 1919. Despite being knocked unconscious, he refused to leave the game and went on to record the final out for the win.

Ouija boards were first produced and sold as a commercial parlor game in 1890 but the technique and method of automatic writing used in the Ouija board is mentioned in writings from China from 1100 AD under the Song dynasty.

All Olympic curling stones come from one Scottish island called Ailsa Craig.

Garrett McNamara holds the record for the largest wave ever surfed, set in November 2011 in Nazare, Portugal. The wave was 78 feet (24 meters) tall.

The modern game of field hockey was developed in England in the 19th century but its roots date back to ancient Egypt.

The only head coach in University of Kansas basketball history with a losing career record is James Naismith, the man who invented basketball.

The first beer mats, or "Bierdeckel," were originally created in Germany in the 19th century to cover the tops of glasses to keep out dust, flies and other insects.

The Russian team arrived 12 days late to the 1908 Olympics in London because they were using the Julian calendar, which was different from the Gregorian calendar that was being used by the organizers of the Olympics.

In 1931, a 17-year-old girl named Jackie Mitchell struck out baseball legends Babe Ruth and Lou Gehrig in an exhibition match. Three days later the baseball commissioner voided her contract and banned women from playing baseball.

Scientists don't know what makes the stones curl across the ice in Olympic curling and despite several studies, it remains an unsolved mystery.

The Whoopee cushion was often employed by 14-year-old Roman Emperor Elagabalus, who used it frequently on guests. He was assassinated at the age of 18.

LANGUAGE

The ampersand symbol (&) is formed from the letters in et—the Latin word for "and".

You are taught in English classes that its 'i before e except after c'. Except there are more words in the English language that break that rule than follow it.

In a 1917 letter to Winston Churchill, Admiral John Fisher used the abbreviation "OMG."

People using sign language also have different dialects and regional variations.

More than eighty cultures around the world speak to each other in whistles.

There are over 6,000 languages in the world but about 2500 are in danger of becoming extinct, while only 23 are used by half the world's population. Mandarin is the most spoken amongst native speakers and English the most spoken overall.

Papa New guinea has more than 830 living languages.

The Bible is the most translated book in the world. It is commonly accepted that the second most translated book is Pinocchio by Carlo Collodi.

The Latin alphabet's origins are over 3000 years old and lay not in Greek, but the Phoenician script created in modern day Lebanon.

There are over 50,000 characters in the Chinese language, but you only need to know 2,500 to 3,000 characters to read a newspaper.

Welsh is spoken in the Patagonia region of Argentina.

Moving each letter of the word 'yes' 16 places up the alphabet spells the French word 'oui'.

The longest word in the English language, according to the Guinness Book of World Records, is pneumonoultramicroscopicsilicovolcanoconiosis.

Piggy banks are not named after pigs but after the old English word for clay, "pygg".

Mano a mano' means hand to hand not man to man.

Every 'c' in Pacific Ocean is pronounced differently.

Oxymoron is an oxymoron. it comes from the Greek oxys, meaning sharp and moronos meaning dull.

Su Hui, a fourth century Chinese poet, wrote a poem called "Xuanji Tu" or "A Picture of the Turning Sphere," in the form of a twenty-nine-by-twenty-nine-character grid. Each line can be read forward, backwards, horizontally, or vertically. The poem is considered to be a masterpiece of Chinese literature.

The use of "X" to represent a kiss in English-speaking countries originated in medieval times when illiterate people would sign documents with an "X" and kiss it to show sincerity and authenticity.

Cursing aloud can increase a person's pain tolerance.

The phrase to win something "hands down" originally referred to a jockey who won a race without whipping his horse or pulling back the reins.

The United States has no official language.

One language dies every fortnight.

Shakespeare invented 1700 words which are still in use today.

"Close, But No Cigar" comes from 1800's fairground games where the prizes were cigars or bottles of whiskey.

A lion cannot be the "king of the Jungle" because lions don't live in the jungle.

A bull in a china shop will actively avoid hitting the shelves.

A rolling stone truly gathers no moss.

"Goodbye" is a modern combination or contraction of "God be with you."

Societies around the world named colors in the same order.

Languages tend to feature more words for "warm" colors such as orange and red than "cool" colors like blue and green.

The color orange was named after the fruit.

Kleptomania was a word invented for the upper class because words like theft and larceny were considered too lowly and it was not considered a valid psychiatric ailment yet.

The word "run" has 645 different meanings in English.

Shampoo comes from the Hindi word meaning "to Knead".

The English alphabet used to have 6 more letters than it does today.

The Korean equivalent to 'Once upon a time' is 'Long ago, when tigers used to smoke'.

The urge to look through people's windows as you pass by their houses is called crytoscopophilia.

Dots that appear above letters such as i and j are called a 'tittle'.

The phrase "pipe dream" comes from the visions seen by smoking opium.

TECHNOLOGY

A modern scientific calculator has six times more processing power than the computer that landed Apollo 11 on the moon.

Bluetooth was named after Viking king Harald Bluetooth because the creators believed the technology would unite devices the way Harald Bluetooth united the tribes of Denmark and Norway.

In 1999 Google's founders, Larry Page and Sergey Brin offered to sell their search engine to Excite. At first, they asked for $1 million but Excite turned them down. So, they lowered their price to $750,00. Excite still said no.

Facebook engineers originally wanted to call the "Like" button the "Awesome" button.

In 1991 scientists at Cambridge all worked in different rooms but shared one coffee pot. So, they set up a camera that was on the network so they could check it wasn't empty before going to fill their cups. Two years later when two members of the team couldn't use the network, they ran the images over the internet instead, creating the world's first webcam. It was retired in 2001 and sold for £3,350.

The first ever email was sent in 1971.

The world's first website, info.cern.ch, is still online.

Recent studies show that 51% of all Internet traffic is generated by non-human sources.

Internet access is legal right In Finland. All citizens have the right to a minimum broadband connection speed of 10Mbps.

72 hours of videos are uploaded on YouTube every minute.

A Swiss study showed that robots programmed to emit a blue light when they found a specific ring evolved to stop emitting the light so that other robots would not find the ring.

Two Facebook AIs developed their own method of talking to each other that programmers could not understand.

Steve Jobs could not write any code.

The AI market is being monopolized by a few large companies.

An AI being studied by researchers from Stanford University and Google intended to transform aerial images into street maps was found to be cheating, by encoding data to evade having to learn to perform a task.

An AI was asked to play an 80's arcade game to see if it could learn new ways to win. It did so by finding a bug in the code and simply used the bug to win every time.

AI will learn to become aggressive to achieve its goals. AI research has shown that AIs will happily use violence against other AI opponents to win a game.

In 2011 the Nautilus supercomputer predicted the location of Osama Bin Laden to within 200km.

An AI called Deep Patient taught itself to become more proficient than doctors at predicting patient illnesses.

AI can now efficiently and effectively put you in any scenario in a video or photograph.

In 1976 Ron Wayne, one of the co-founders of Apple sold his shares for $800. Today they would be worth $35 billion.

The startup music for Microsoft's Windows 95 was composed on an Apple Mac.

Jeff Bezos, founder, and CEO of Amazon, has an estranged father who was a unicyclist in a circus.

Teflon was on sale from 1946 and wasn't a result of the space program.

The research that created Google was funded by grants from the CIA.

According to Nintendo, Mario is not a plumber.

There are computers for the Amish, which have no internet, videos, or music.

Surgeons who play video games at least 3 hours a week perform 27% faster and make 37% fewer errors.

In 2001, Beaver College changed its name to Arcadia, in part because anti-porn filters blocked access to the school's website.

Bar code scanners read the white space between the black lines rather than the black lines themselves.

Bridgeville, California (population of 25) was the first town to be sold on eBay in 2002 and has been up for sale 3 times since.

Mark Zuckerberg suffers from red-green color blindness which is why the primary color on Facebook is blue.

The first woman to earn a PhD in Computer Science in the United States was Mary Kenneth Keller, in 1965. She also earned a master's degree in mathematics and physics and helped develop computer programming languages. She was also a Catholic nun.

If you point your car's key fob to your head, it increases the remote's signal range.

The oldest webcam still streaming today is The San Francisco FogCam which has been operational since 1994.

The video game Grand Theft Auto V has made more money than any movie in history.

There is a lightbulb located at 4550 East Avenue, Livermore, California, and maintained by the Livermore-Pleasanton Fire Department called the Centennial Light. It is the world's longest-lasting light bulb, burning since 1901 and has almost never been turned off.

The Twitter bird's official name was Larry.

A study in 2016 found that, on average, any two Facebook users are only 3.57 degrees of separation apart.

The nation of Tuvalu earns over 10% of its gross national income from licensing its .tv internet domain.

Bill Gates was so addicted to Minesweeper, he used to sneak into then-Microsoft President Michael Hallman's office to play it, as he had uninstalled the game on his computer.

In 1979 a group of former Atari employees formed another games company and called it Activision so it would be listed alphabetically before Atari in the phone book. Two of those founders left Activision and founded Accolade, named so it would be listed alphabetically before Atari and Activision. Another two employees then left Activision and started their own games company and called it Acclaim, named so it would be listed alphabetically before Atari, Activision, and Accolade.

INVENTIONS

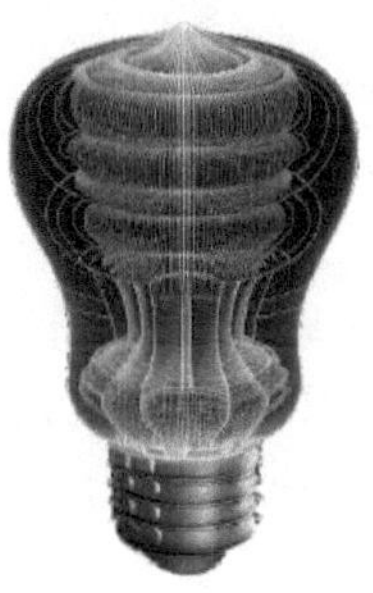

An archaeological dig in Peru in the 1930s discovered the first known telephone, made by the Chimu people in 820AD and is described as a marvel of acoustic engineering.

Scotsman Alexander Bain invented the fax machine using discarded mechanisms from clocks in 1843.

Robert Cornelius set up a camera to take a picture of himself and then ran into frame, taking the first ever selfie in 1881.

The Phonautograph, invented by Édouard-Léon Scott de Martinville in 1860, was the first invention to record sound.

German ophthalmologist Adolf Gaston Eugen
Fick fabricated the first successful afocal scleral
contact lens in 1888.

British inventor Kane Kramer invented the first
digital music player, called the IXI, in 1979.

Heron of Alexandria invented the first vending
machine made to dispense holy water to pilgrims
visiting a temple in 61AD.

Heron of Alexandria also invented the first
known steam engine, called the Aeolipile. It used
steam to spin a sphere on its axis.

The first documented users of paper in the toilet
are the Chinese in 589AD.

The oldest historical records of people using forks date from the Bronze Age and were found in Gansu, a north-central province of China.

The first person to build a camera and whose work directly led to the invention of the photographic camera was an Arab Physicist called Hasan Ibn Al-Haytham who invented the pinhole camera in 1021AD.

The first 3D movie, called "The Power of Love," was shown in Los Angeles in 1922.

The first feature-length film captured in natural color rather than using colorization techniques was a documentary called "With Our King and Queen Through India" in 1912.

The earliest evidence of anything resembling modern ice cream comes from the Tang period of China (618AD - 907AD).

The first patent for an automatic door was filed in 1904 by Canadian inventor Dee Horton.

The first known seismoscope used to detect and measure earthquakes was invented in China during the 2nd century AD by a scientist named Zhang Heng.

The first ever escalator was installed at the Old Iron Pier at Coney Island amusement park in New York City in 1896.

The first submarine was built in 1620 by a Dutch inventor named Cornelis Drebbel. Made of wood and covered in leather it was designed to be propelled by oars and is believed to have been able to stay submerged for several hours at a time.

Flamethrowers were first deployed by the Byzantium Empire in the 7th century AD.

The invention of the carbonated soft drink started in 1767 when Joseph Priestley discovered a way of infusing water with carbon dioxide, inventing soda water.

Brain surgery was performed in the Neolithic period, as long ago as 10,000 BCE and we know that people survived the procedure.

The first known use of cardboard-like material was invented in China over 2000 years ago. Known as "zhi," it was made from a combination of mulberry bark and rice straw.

The tea bag was invented by accident. In 1908 tea merchant Thomas Sullivan distributed his tea samples in small, silken bags. His customers, not understanding that these were samples, simply dunked them in hot water and suddenly Sullivan was swamped with orders for his 'tea bags'.

The bendy straw was invented for use by patients in hospitals.

The tin can was invented in 1810 by Peter Durand. The can opener wasn't invented until 1870 by William Lyman.

Brazilian Alfredo Moser invented a lamp in 2002 that uses plastic bottles filled with water and a small amount of bleach pushed through a hole in the roof. The water in the bottles refracts the sunlight, creating a source of light that can be used during the day without the need for electricity, and the bleach stops algae growing in the bottle. The illumination produced is equal to a 60-watt bulb.

The toothbrush was invented in 1498 in China, during the Ming Dynasty. Made from bamboo or animal bone with animal hairs as bristles.

The first music streaming service started in 1897. Users in New York could pick up their phones and connect to the Telharmonium, a central hub that would pipe music being played live by two musicians playing 24 hours a day.

When chemist Constantin Fahlberg ate his lunch without washing his hands, he noticed the rolls he was eating tasted sweet. He traced the sweetness back to the benzoic sulfimide he had been working with and in 1878 discovered Saccharin.

Thomas Edison invented the light bulb, but his invention would have been a failure had another inventor, Lewis Latimer, not come up with a solution that made the lightbulbs cheaper, long lasting, and more efficient.

When Robert Taylor came up with the idea of putting liquid soap in a pump bottle, he wanted to make sure big companies didn't steal his idea. So, he bought about 100 million pump bottles from the only two manufacturers in the US, giving him a year's head start.

Bubble wrap was invented in 1957 by Alfred Fielding and Marc Chavannes by sealing two shower curtains together. They originally tried to sell it as wallpaper.

The microwave was invented after its inventor, Percy Spencer, noticed that a chocolate bar melted in his pocket while he was working on a new type of vacuum tube used in radar equipment, called a magnetron.

Johann Wolfgang Döbereiner was a German chemist who invented a non-portable lighter in 1823, three years before the invention of the match.

When Anders Celsius invented the temperature scale, he put 100° as the point for freezing and 0° as the point for boiling.

Safety Glass was first invented when French chemist Édouard Bénédictus accidentally knocked a flask off his desk that didn't shatter because it contained plastic cellulose nitrate.

TASER is an acronym that stands for "Thomas A. Swift's Electric Rifle", in reference to a character in a series of adventure novels.

The first electric vehicle was created in 1832 by Scottish inventor Robert Anderson.

Cruise control on cars was invented in 1948 by blind inventor and mechanical engineer Ralph Teetor.

The First power windows were fitted in cars
1946.

Ludvig Nobel, brother of Alfred Nobel (founder
of the Nobel Prize and inventor of dynamite)
invented oil tankers and much of the science
needed to transport oil by ship. He refused to
patent any part of his invention.

Dry cleaning was accidentally invented in 1855
when a French maid knocked over a kerosene
lamp onto a dirty tablecloth and the owner
noticed the tablecloth was cleaner after the spill.

ART & LITERATURE

Fabergé, famous for his eggs, also once made a Fabergé potato.

The oldest known version of the Cinderella story is the ancient Greek story of Rhodopis, a Greek courtesan in Egypt, who loses a sandal which is found by the king.

Artist Salvador Dalí would often get out of paying for drinks and meals by drawing on the checks, making them priceless works of art and therefore un-cashable.

In J.M. Barrie's novel Peter and Wendy, he writes that the number of the 'lost boys' changes and that Peter Pan "thins them out" when they start to grow up 'which is against the rules', implying that Peter Pan kills them.

The first real murder on the Orient Express occurred in 1936, two years after the novel was published. It remains unsolved.

Mary Shelley wrote Frankenstein at 18, because she was competing with Lord Byron on who could write the best horror story.

Jack H. Hetherington was writing a paper in 1975 when he realized he had written the entire thing in the plural despite being the only author. Rather than going back to edit the whole piece, he simply added a second author, F.D.C. Willard, otherwise known as his cat, Chester.

During his entire life, Vincent Van Gogh sold exactly one painting, "Red Vineyard at Arles".

The owner of the Café de la Rotonde in Paris would allow starving artists to pay for their drinks with a painting or drawing. In the early 20th century, the walls of the cafe would have been casually adorned with works now considered priceless including work by Pablo Picasso.

Kunsten Museum of Modern Art lent an artist $84,000 in cash to use in a re-creation of a piece he had made before. He delivered two blank canvases and titled them "Take the Money and Run".

The largest museum in the world in terms of objects displayed is the Hermitage Museum in Saint Petersburg, Russia. If you spent a minute on every piece, it would take you 11 years to look at everything the museum has to offer.

Agatha Christie was a very keen surfer.

Actor James Franco was behind a project called the Museum of Non-Visible Art. The project created an invisible sculpture called 'Fresh Air', described as an endless supply of oxygen. Someone bought the 'sculpture' for $10,000.

Han van Meegeren was a legendary art forger who is believed to have duped buyers out of millions of dollars. He became national hero in the Netherlands after World War II when it was discovered that he had cheated Hermann Göring out of over a million guilders.

Michelangelo hid under the Medici Chapel in Florence for three months during a period of political turmoil, occupying his time by sketching on the walls with charcoal. His whereabouts were a secret for almost 500 years until the museum director stumbled upon the drawings in 1976.

Deadline is a science fiction short story written in 1944 about a group of scientists working on a bomb. It includes topics such as uranium enrichment and methods of isotopic separation. It had so much detail that the government were convinced its author, Cleve Cartmill, had access to classified information about the Manhattan Project, the top-secret effort to develop the first atomic bomb during World War II.

Michael Richards, an American artist, created a sculpture titled "Tar Baby vs. St. Sebastian," which features a life-size cast of his body and instead of arrows, had planes flying into his body. The airplanes represent the violence and destruction of war and terrorism. Richards died on the 92nd floor of Tower One on 9/11.

One of the most famous mimes of the 20th century, Marcel Marceau, released a record entitled 'The Best of Marcel Marceau'. It was nothing more than 38 minutes of complete silence followed by thunderous applause.

Prior to the first nuclear bomb detonation in July of 1945, isotopes strontium-90 and cesium-137 did not exist in nature. Pieces of art and bottles of wine claimed to pre-date 1945 can be authenticated by testing for cesium.

Pain levels are reduced by up to 33% when looking at a painting we consider to be beautiful.

Jiminy Cricket is flattened against a wall by Pinocchio with a hammer in the original Italian story by Carlo Collodi.

"Who's Who in the CIA" was a book published in East Berlin during the height of the Cold War by the Stasi. The book is now nearly impossible to find and even has a habit of disappearing from U.S. libraries.

A. A. Milne wrote Winnie the Pooh as a lighthearted distraction from his PTSD which was so severe it could be set off by buzzing bees.

Sir Arthur Conan Doyle, the creator of Sherlock Holmes, was a founder and played goalkeeper for the amateur Portsmouth Association Football Club.

When the Mona Lisa was stolen from the Louvre in 1911, the empty space it left on the wall attracted more visitors than the painting had.

Police investigating the theft of the Mona Lisa had Pablo Picasso as a prime suspect.

The Monster in Frankenstein is never named.

The Mona Lisa has no eyebrows. She originally did but years of cleaning and poor restoration work have caused them to fade.

Le Bateau' By Henri Matisse Was Hung Upside Down at The Museum of Modern Art in New York in 1961. It was 47 days before anyone noticed.

Roman statues were commissioned with detachable heads, just in case.

The first pencil factory was established in Keswick, England in 1565.

There are five versions of The Scream by Edvard Munch.

In The Scream by Edvard Munch, no one knows if the figure is screaming or reacting to the scream of nature.

Harry Potter was rejected by 12 different publishing houses.

Gainsborough used broccoli as models for his outdoor scenes.

Monet paid his gardener to dust off his water lilies before painting them.

Van Gogh's "Olive Trees" has a dead grasshopper embedded in the paint in the lower foreground.

Some buildings in Hong Kong have large holes designed for dragons to fly through.

Early sketches by the designer Frédéric-Auguste Bartholdi, hint that the Statue of Liberty was originally intended to be a Muslim woman at the Entrance to the Suez Canal.

There is a Museum of Bad Art in Somerville, Massachusetts in the United States. It exhibits 'art too bad to be ignored'.

The Eiffel Tower was designed and built by Gustave Eiffel for the 1889 World's Fair in Paris, France and was only meant to be a temporary structure.

The oldest confirmed statues are small figurines called the "Venus of Hohle Fels" and the "Lion-man of Hohlenstein-Stadel" both of which were discovered in caves in Germany and are estimated to be at least 35,000 years old, created by the prehistoric Aurignacian culture.

The most expensive painting ever sold is Leonardo da Vinci's Salvator Mundi, circa 1490–1500 which sold for $450.3 million at Christie's in November 2017.

Picasso fired blanks at people who bored him.

Ian Fleming, creator of James Bond novels, went to school in the UK, near an area called Spyway, next to the estate of the Bond family whose motto is 'Non Suffict Orbis,' which means 'The World Is Not Enough.' The family had a famous spy in the Elizabethan era called John Bond.

RELIGION

Adam and Eve eat the forbidden fruit from the tree of knowledge. The Old Testament never says it was an apple nor does it mention what it was.

According to a fragment from 'Papyrus 115', discovered at Oxford University's Ashmolean Museum and the oldest manuscript (about 1,700 years old) of Revelation 13, the number of the beast is in fact 616.

Noah did not take two of each animal on the Ark. God tells Noah to take with him seven pairs of clean animals, seven pairs of all birds, and one pair of each unclean animal.

We do not know how many Wise Men came to see Jesus, only that they brought three gifts.

Jonah is swallowed by a 'big fish', not a whale, which would have been unable to swallow anything as large as a human.

The phrase "Money is the root of all evil" does not exist in the Bible. The verse in I Timothy 6:10 says, "the love of money is a root of all kinds of evil".

Nowhere in any religious books is the devil described to be looking any different than the other angels. Attempts to associate the devil with pagan gods and animals transformed the look of the devil to what we see today.

In the Abrahamic religions, Angels are not cherubs with wings, but non-corporeal beings made of energy or light.

Jesus was not born in a stable.

The Vatican Bank is the world's only bank that allows ATM users to perform transactions in Latin.

In 20860, the Christian and Islamic calendars will match.

Santa Claus was a real man. Saint Nicholas was a monk in the third century who was well known for his kindness. The name came from Dutch immigrants to the US who referred to him as Sinterklaas.

Saint Patrick was not Irish. His birthplace is debated as to being Scotland or Wales.

The Pope has eight official titles: Bishop of Rome, Vicar of Jesus Christ, Successor of the Prince of the Apostles, Supreme Pontiff of the Universal Church, Primate of Italy, Archbishop and Metropolitan of the Roman Province, Sovereign of the State of Vatican City, Servant of the Servants of God. The one official title he does not have is 'Pope'.

In 1631, Robert Barkerand Martin Lucas, the royal printers in London, published what was meant to be a reprint of the King James Bible. However, a mistake in the printing process led to the word "not" being omitted from the seventh of the ten Commandments, "thou shall not commit adultery." This version, now known as 'The Wicked Bible,' has sixteen known copies left and has become a collector's item.

The term "devil's advocate" was originally given to the church official appointed to argue against a candidate for sainthood.

During the French Revolution, France established a state-sponsored atheistic religion called the Cult of Reason to replace Catholicism. It only lasted about a year and was later banned by Napoleon.

Residents of Shingo, Japan, believe Jesus did not die on a cross but instead fled to their town and became a rice farmer.

Mount Athos, Greece, is an entirely self-governed peninsula inhabited only by Orthodox monks. Female humans and animals are banned from entry except for female cats which are explicitly permitted to keep mice out.

Easter is named after a pagan goddess of spring called Eoster.

Biblical accounts of Joseph and the drought sets the story in Egypt around 3600 years ago. Studies of ice cores on Mount Kilimanjaro in Tanzania, have revealed that a drought did take place around that time in the area.

When the Pope visited Arizona in 1987, 75,000 attended Mass at a local university's stadium. The name of the stadium and the image of the mascot had to be covered because their mascot is the devil holding a pitchfork and the stadium's name was Sun Devil Stadium.

An obscure rule from 1917 Roman Catholic canon states that "any newly discovered territory would fall under the bishopric from whence the discovering expedition departed." Which makes the bishop of Orlando also Bishop of the Moon.

Pope Francis used to be a bouncer at a bar.

There is a wooden ladder placed against the wall of Church of the Holy Sepulcher in Jerusalem that cannot be moved due to an agreement between the six ecumenical Christian orders that no cleric may move, rearrange, or alter any property without the consent of all six orders. No one is sure who put the ladder there, and more importantly, to which sect they belonged. No one knows when it was placed there but an engraving exists from 1728 showing the ladder.

"If a man really wanted to make a million dollars, the best way to do it would be to start his own religion" said L Ron Hubbard in 1948. Seven years later he founded Scientology.

SCIENCE

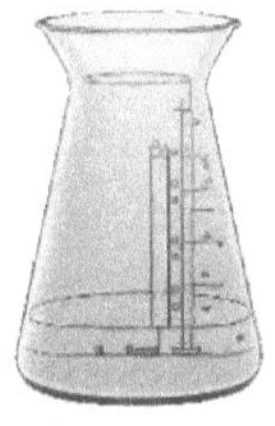

Using a petrol driven lawnmower for one hour produces more pollutants than six cars will create in that same hour, or one car will produce in a 100-mile car trip.

In 2019 MIT engineers took the lead in producing the blackest black. Made from vertically aligned carbon nanotubes, it captures at least 99.995% of incoming light beating the previous claimant by 0.035%.

Hot water freezes more quickly than cold water. The principle is called the Mpemba effect, but science hasn't come to an agreement on why it happens. The Inverse Mpemba effect, where cold water heats up faster than hot water, also exists but is far less noticeable.

There are over twenty known states of matter.

The Nobel Peace Prize was created in 1895 by
the man who invented dynamite.

A clock on the International Space Station is
slower than a clock on Earth.

Einstein did not fail math or physics.

Leucippus and his student Democritus first wrote
in the 5th-century BC that all matter is composed
of small, indivisible particles, which they called
atoms.

The dinosaurs became extinct four million years
before the period that formed the Rocky
Mountains and the Alps.

Quantum entanglement is a bizarre phenomenon where two particles can be intimately linked to each other even if separated by billions of light-years of space. Despite their vast separation, a change induced in one will affect the other.

There is a state that some substances can reach called the Triple Point where the material will exist as solid, liquid and gas at once but only at a specific temperature and pressure.

Oxygen is colorless when in a gaseous state but as a liquid or solid it is pale blue.

The Eiffel Tower can be 15 cm taller during the summer due to thermal expansion.

Sitting too close to the television will not damage your eyesight. The myth evolved from the fact that some early color TVs emitted low levels of radiation.

The speed of light changes depending on the medium it is travelling through. It can only travel at its maximum speed of 186,282 miles per second in the vacuum of space but through air, water, and glass it will slow down by the refractive index of what it is passing through.

Around a million, billion neutrinos from the Sun will pass through your body while you read this sentence.

…and now they are already past the Moon.

Astatine is the rarest naturally occurring element with less than one gram present at any given time in the Earth's crust. The properties of astatine are unknown because it only exists for less than a second.

A hydrogen atom has a mass that is less than the sum of its constituent particles.

The phrase "plastic surgery" is derived from the Greek word "plasteo," which means "shape" and not because of any substance used in the procedure.

Non-Newtonian fluids are fluids that can behave as liquids or solids depending on the force exerted on them. If you walk slowly on a non-Newtonian fluid it will behave like a liquid but if you run it will behave like a solid.

At -40°, Celsius and Fahrenheit are the same temperature.

No one knows why we cry in emotional circumstances.

Velociraptors in Jurassic Park are tall, intelligent, scaly pack hunters. In reality, they were about the size of a chicken, feathered and hunted alone. For a dinosaur they were smart, but that just means smarter than a rabbit but not as smart as a cat or dog.

No one knows how general anesthesia works.

No one knows how and why animals migrate back to their place of birth.

No one knows how turbulence happens.

No one knows how bicycles stay upright. Gyroscopic forces are believed to play a role, but they are not the only factor.

We know a lot about why ice is slippery but not all aspects of this phenomenon have been explained.

The first person known to advance a theory of evolution was an Arab scientist by the name of al-Basri in the 9th century, a thousand years before Darwin. His writings introduced the principles and mechanisms of natural selection.

You will not sink in quicksand.

The presence of a picture of an eye reduces unethical behavior.

When a leaf gets eaten, it warns other leaves.

Scientists at the University of Richmond in the US trained rats to drive tiny cars by giving treats as a reward. The rats ended up loving driving so much they would do it without a reward.

Various studies have shown that coffee prevents cancer, causes cancer, makes you live longer, makes you die younger and reduces your risk of diabetes.

There is no direct evidence that dinosaurs could roar.

The inventor of leaded gasoline once argued that leaded gasoline was perfectly safe, by pouring it onto his hands, and then putting a bottle of it under his nose and inhaling it for 60 seconds. He then had to leave work after being diagnosed with lead poisoning. He went on to invent Freon, a CFC that was later banned after being shown to be responsible for ozone depletion. Then he got polio, so he invented a pulley system that let him pull himself out of bed. He died after becoming entangled in his invention and being strangled.

Researchers at the Bureau of Alcohol, Tobacco and Firearms research laboratory in Beltsville, Maryland in the US tried to ignite gasoline with a cigarette more than 2000 times and in every single attempt the gasoline did not ignite.

A car can skip across a body of water on to the other side, if the angle and speed are correct, much like a pebble will skim across water.

In 1927, Thomas Parnell, Professor of Physics at the University of Queensland in Australia, started what has become longest-running laboratory experiment ever when he heated a sample of pitch and poured it into a glass funnel to demonstrate that some substances which appear solid are highly viscous fluids. Two drops of pitch fell before he died in 1947. No-one witnessed either of them. There have been seven drops since, all of which have also not been witnessed. One happened while the professor in charge of it when to get some tea. And even when a webcam was installed, the eighth drop fell just after the webcam went down with technical issues. The last drop occurred in 2014 and was missed because maintenance was being done to the experiment.

J.J. Thomson won the Nobel in Physics in 1906 when he showed electrons were particles. His son won it in 1937 for showing that electrons are waves. They were both right because electrons have wave-particle duality meaning they can exhibit either condition depending on experimental conditions.

In 1898 Bayer introduced diacetylmorphine, marketed as a cure for morphine addiction and cough suppressant. The drug is better known today as heroin.

Rubbing your hands on stainless steel while under running water can help neutralize the odor-causing compounds of onion and garlic.

Before refrigeration, Russians dropped live brown frogs into their milk to keep it from spoiling. Recent research at Moscow State University in Russia, has shown the amphibians' skin has antimicrobial compounds as potent against Salmonella and Staphylococcus bacteria as prescription antibiotics.

A bullet fired horizontally will land at the same time as a bullet dropped as long as both are released from the same height.

It may be possible to dodge a bullet from a sniper rife that is over 500 yards (457 m) away if you see the muzzle flash.

Going outside without a coat with wet hair will not make you sick but can lead to changes in the body that weaken the immune system, making you more prone to illness.

At the Orfield Laboratories in Minnesota, there is an anechoic chamber, a specialized room that is designed to completely absorb sound waves, which is the quietest place in the world. It has a measured sound level of -9.4 decibels. It is so quiet that some people report hearing their lungs.

Chewing gum boosts mental proficiency and is considered a better test aid than caffeine.

A sailboat stranded in calm water can move forward using an on-board fan to blow air into its own sail.

A motion detector can be fooled by moving very slowly or by holding a bed sheet in front of you.

Concrete is stronger if fibers from carrots are added to it.

Swimming after eating is not dangerous. The earliest known version of the myth comes from a scout handbook published in 1908.

Some cacti can move more of themselves underground if it gets too hot.

Mathematically, folding a piece of paper only forty-two times would make it thick enough to reach the moon.

Researchers have discovered that small concentrations of Viagra, when dissolved in water, can make cut-flowers stay erect for up to a week longer than they usually would.

The caps of ball point pens have holes at the top to prevent suffocation if swallowed.

Orchids suffer from jetlag. After a long journey a plant that usually opens its leaves in the morning will open its leaves at night and will take a few days to readjust.

Researchers have been able to create a new phase of water ice, which they dubbed "superionic ice" or "hot ice". It is believed to be common inside frozen planets like Uranus and Neptune and has properties of both liquid and solid.

A survey, by Brent Helliker and Suzanna Richter from the University of Pennsylvania, of 39 trees across a range of environments from the frozen north to the balmy south of North America, found that both deciduous and evergreen species across the entire continent manage to maintain the temperature of their leaves at an average of 21°C over the course of a year, the ideal temperature for photosynthesis.

Brass doorknobs have a natural ability to disinfect themselves through a process called the oligodynamic effect, where the metal releases ions, such as copper or zinc ions, which are toxic to microbes.

The Pisonia tree lures birds to their death by emitting a glue-like substance that traps the birds on its branches. No one really knows why.

In 1999 scientists working off the coast of Namibia discovered a bacterium called Thiomargarita namibiensis whose individual cells can grow up to 0.75mm wide, which is big enough for you to see it without a microscope.

The theory that using a cell phone while pumping gas is dangerous has been tested and debunked numerous times. No-one is even sure why the signs to not use cell phones at gas stations were put up in the first place.

There is a scientific scale to categorize the seven different types of bowel movements one can have and it is called the Bristol Stool Scale.

You can treat jellyfish stings with shaving foam
and a credit card, but vinegar, alcohol or urine
will only make things worse.

A Formula One car generates enough downforce
to drive upside down in a tunnel at high speed.

The first car ever to break the 100kph (62mph)
barrier was an electric car. The 1899 speed record
of La Jamais Contente of 105.882 km/h (65.792
mph) held for three years.

Treating a wound with maggots can save a limb
from amputation. Almost 10 percent of people
would rather have their limb amputated than
have maggots applied to it.

Dr William Frankland created the hygiene hypothesis and the pollen count, worked as an assistant to Alexander Fleming in the development of penicillin, treated Saddam Hussein for asthma and published his last paper at the age of 104.

COMMERCE

Samsung, the largest business conglomerate in South Korea, began as a company trading in groceries and noodles.

The founders of Samsung and LG, Lee and Koo, were close friends at elementary school.

Sega was started by two Americans and is an abbreviation of Service Games.

The ash produced by coal-fired plants is more radioactive than the waste from nuclear power plants.

56% of pilots admit to falling asleep. 29% say they woke up to find the co-pilot asleep.

Due to its happy meals, McDonalds is the world's largest toy distributor.

Subliminal advertising does not work.

Classical music in a restaurant can increase the amount people spend on wine. This is known as the "Mozart Effect".

Until 1996 Marvel owned the rights to the word "Zombie".

Federal Reserve Bank and central banks across the world burn worn out bills to produce electricity.

Nishiyama Onsen Keiunkan is the world's oldest hotel and has been in business since 705A.D.

Ma Yu Ching's Bucket Chicken House in Kaifeng, China is considered the world's oldest operating restaurant, first opening in 1153 AD during the Jing Dynasty. It is known for its specialty dish, "Kaifeng Bucket Chicken".

After racking up a $40 late fee on a copy of Apollo 13 at Blockbuster, the defunct video rental store, Reed Hastings was inspired to start Netflix. Three years later, in the year 2000, he offered to sell Netflix to Blockbuster for $50 million.

Lamborghini originally manufactured tractors. Ferruccio Lamborghini started making sports cars after being insulted by Enzo Ferrari.

The world's oldest surviving bank is "Banca Monte dei Paschi di Siena," which was founded in 1472 and is currently Italy's 3rd largest bank.

When three-letter airport codes became standard, airports that had been using two letters simply added an X.

Until 29 October 2018, you could fly Finnair from Copenhagen to Helsinki on flight number 666. The code name for Helsinki airport is HEL.

In 1986 12 jurors in Florida got stuck in an elevator serviced by the Otis Elevator company for twenty minutes. They were on their way to a lawsuit against the Otis elevator company.

80% of "Close Door" buttons in lifts do not do anything as the doors are on a timer.

Volvo gave away the patent for seatbelts because they felt it was more important to save lives.

Ferdinand Porsche's first car design was for an called the Egger-Lohner C.2 Phaeton model in 1898 and it was an electric car.

The first Ford Mustang (Serial #000001) was accidentally sold to pilot Captain Stanley Tucker. It was meant to be for display only as it was pre-production version.

Volkswagen sells about one million more sausages that it produces than cars it produces.

The most expensive car ever sold was a 1955 Mercedes-Benz 300 SLR Uhlenhaut Coupe for $143,000,000. It was sold at a Sotheby's auction in May 2022.

Around 65% of all Rolls-Royce cars ever built are still on the road today.

Up to the 1970's, humans were being used as crash test dummies in Germany.

More than 60% of the world's commercial seed market is controlled by just four companies.

Palm oil is in up to 50% of packaged products in supermarkets.

Los Angeles once had one of the largest electric rail systems in the world. American automobile, tire, and oil companies worked together to bring it down along with mass transit systems in 44 other US cities.

On January 29, 1886, Carl Benz filed his patent application for his "motor car with gas engine operation". The German public were dubious and did not trust his invention. His wife, Bertha Benz, saved the entire motor car industry when in August of 1888 she travelled 100 kilometers from Mannheim to Pforzheim with their two sons Richard and Eugen, without her husband's knowledge. She changed people's perspective on the motor car almost overnight.

In 1915 farmer Tom Lyle Williams witnessed his sister Mabel applying mascara, which was a mixture of coal dust and Vaseline at the time, to her eyelashes to enhance their appearance and thought he could make a better product. He named his product "Maybelline" after his sister.

Mary Quant, who is widely credited with popularizing the miniskirt, says she named it after the Mini Cooper car and not after the skirt's size.

In 2018, the United States Patent and Trademark Office granted a trademark for the smell of Play-Doh.

There is a 20-mile radius around Mattoon, Illinois in the USA where Burger King cannot open a store as there was already a restaurant there named Burger King that has been awarded the rights to the name in the area.

The name "Jeep" derives from the military term "GP", which stands for "General Purpose" vehicle. The GP vehicle was a light 4-wheel drive vehicle that was used by the US military during World War II and often pronounced as "jeep" by military personnel.

The most popular car color is white.

MYSTERIES, COINCIDENCES & CONSPIRACIES

There are several coincidences between the assassinations of President John F. Kennedy and Abraham Lincoln. Both were shot on a Friday, in the back of the head, sitting next to their wives by men who would die before going on trial. Lincoln was shot in Ford's Theatre, Kennedy in a Ford Lincoln.

In 1992, German toxicologist Svetlana Balabanova discovered traces of cocaine on an Egyptian mummy called Henut Taui's hair as well as on the hair of several other mummies at the State Museum of Egyptian Art in Munich, Germany. The only source of cocaine at that time was the coca plants native to the Americas.

In July 1975 Erskine Ebbin was knocked down and killed by a taxi driver while riding a moped in Hamilton, Bermuda. Nearly a year earlier, the same taxi driver, carrying the same passenger, had knocked down and killed Neville Ebbin, Erskin's brother, on the same road while riding the same moped.

In January 1925, the large light bulb manufacturers in the United States and Europe formed the Phoebus Cartel. It regulated competition so that American and European manufacturers wouldn't compete in their respective markets and agreed to lower the life expectancy of light bulbs as the current manufacturing process meant bulbs were lasting too long. This was the first example of corporations creating planned obsolescence into their products.

There is an iron pillar in Delhi, India that is over 7 meters high (over 23 feet) and weighs more than 6 tons. It was constructed between 375AD and 415AD and despite being over a thousand years old has no rust or corrosion on it at all.

In 1561 and five years later in 1566 there were mass sightings of orbs, spheres, cylinders, and a large black triangular object over the skies of Nuremberg, Germany and Basel, Switzerland.

For twenty years, between 1953 and 1973 the US Central Intelligence Agency ran an illegal human experimentation program to test and develop drugs that could be used on individuals to brainwash or torture psychologically. Tests were done on a variety of subjects, both consensually and non-consensually, in the US, Canada and various other countries. Most records were destroyed by the CIA so many details will never be known but the Project was called MKUltra.

In 2001 the American public learned of Operation Northwoods, a proposed false flag operation against American citizens proposed by the US Department of Defense in 1962. It called for CIA operatives to stage and commit acts of violent terrorism against American military and civilian targets, blaming them on the Cuban government, and using it to justify a war against Cuba. It was authorized by the Joint Chiefs of Staff but was stopped by President Kennedy.

There is an annual event that takes place in the months of May to July every year in the city of Yoro, Honduras known as "The Rain of Fish," or Lluvia de Peces. During this event, fish fall from the sky during heavy rainfall.

On December 24, 1945, a fire destroyed the Sodder residence in Fayetteville, West Virginia, United States. George Sodder, his wife Jenn and four of their nine children escaped. The other five were assumed dead in the fire. However, when the blaze was put out, no bodies or evidence of bodies was found in the ashes.

There are a number of elliptical or circular depressions along the east coast of the United States, stretching from coastal New York state to Florida referred to as the Carolina Bays. They are usually marshy and have sandy rims. Their origin is still a mystery to geologists.

Since the 1990's a number of residents of the New Mexico town of Taos have reported hearing a hum of unknown origin that is described as a low-frequency vibration. It could not be picked up by any testing equipment and despite significant attention from the scientific community and several studies, no definitive explanation has been found.

The United States National Oceanic and Atmospheric Administration's Equatorial Pacific Ocean hydrophone array is an underwater listening system that has picked up a number of unidentified sounds that have been given names like Bloop, Upsweep, Train, Julia and Whistle. Other water-based sounds have been heard by humans including "The Ping", heard around Fury and Hecla Strait in Northern Canada, which local fisherman claimed scared away all the marine life.

There have been numerous accounts and recordings of strange sounds coming from the sky, sometimes referred to as 'sky quakes'. They have been reported across the world dating back as far as 1824. No explanation has been found and there are numerous hypotheses trying to explain the phenomenon.

During the 1969 Apollo 10 mission, astronauts Eugene Cernan and John Young were recorded discussing what they described as "outer-space-type music" while flying on the far side of the moon. NASA claimed it was radio interference.

Edward Leedskalnin, a man with a fourth-grade education, built the Coral Castle in Miami-Dade County, Florida in the United States by himself using over 1,100 tons of coral rock and only hand tools. When asked how, his reply was that he understood the laws of weight and leverage.

The Forest Grove Sound was an unexplained noise, described as a "mechanical scream", heard in Forest Grove, Oregon in February 2016. The high-pitched noise was heard intermittently at night and lasted from ten seconds to several minutes at a time. Despite numerous investigations by the Department of Forestry and the Fire Department, no source could be found. Mapping the reports of the noise did not suggest a single location for the source. After February 27 of 2016, the noise disappeared.

There is what is believed to be an individual whale, that has been heard but never sighted since the late 1980s, that calls at the frequency of 50-52 hertz. This pitch is at a higher frequency than that of other whale species.

In January 1900, a relief boat docked at the Scottish Island of Eilean Mor expecting to be met by the three lighthouse keepers, its only inhabitants. But all three men had disappeared and no trace of them was ever found.

There are some strange radio stations on the air but few as strange as number stations and mystery stations. Number stations are shortwave stations that simply broadcast a set of numbers, some at timed schedules, some randomly. The mystery stations, given names by enthusiasts like 'the Buzzer', 'the PIP' and 'the Squeaky Wheel', are known to be Russian and will broadcast random noises, numbers, letters or messages. Sometimes what is broadcast seems accidental.

There is a cup in the British Museum in London, England called the Lycurgus Cup. It is a 4th-century Roman glass cage cup made of a dichroic glass, which shows a different color depending on whether light is passing through it: Red when lit from behind and green when lit from in front. This effect is created by nanoparticles of gold and silver inside the glass, although whether Roman glass makers did this on purpose and how they employed nanotechnology remains a mystery.

On August 7, 1994, a resident of Oakville, Washington in the United States reported that a translucent, gelatinous substance had rained down in the night. The substance, colloquially known as "Oakville blobs," appeared again five more times over the next three weeks. No theory on their origin has ever been proven to be correct. A related substance that is sometimes found on the ground, on trees, or on other surfaces is often referred to as star jelly. It is also a translucent, gooey substance that can be clear, white, yellow, or brown and its origins also remain a mystery.

The assassination of Archduke Ferdinand and his wife was the catalyst that led to the start of World War one. The car he was riding when he was shot carried the number plate AIII 118. Or read another way, 11 November 1918, the actual date for Armistice Day, which is represented by the A.

In an 1838 Edgar Allan Poe book, four survivors
of a sinking draw lots to see who would be eaten.
The loser was the cabin boy who was called
Richard Parker. Forty-six years later a real ship,
called the Mignonette, sank with 4 survivors who
drew lots and ate their cabin boy. His name was
Richard Parker.

Morgan Robertson wrote The Wreck of the
Titan, about an "unsinkable" liner called "The
Titan" that was around 800 ft long, that hit an
iceberg on the starboard side, in the Atlantic, in
April, around 12am, four hundred miles from
Newfoundland at 25 knots and in the story most
of the passengers and crew die because there
were not enough lifeboats. Robertson wrote this
book in 1898, fourteen years before the sinking
of the 882ft Titanic, which hit an iceberg on the
starboard side, in the Atlantic, in April, around
12am, about four hundred miles from
Newfoundland at almost 25 knots and most of
the passengers and crew died because there were
not enough lifeboats.

www.ingramcontent.com/pod-product-compliance
Lightning Source LLC
Chambersburg PA
CBHW051040250726
48656CB00001B/68